FORTY-TWO YEARS AMONGST THE INDIANS AND ESKIMO

FORTY-TWO YEARS
AMONGST THE
INDIANS AND ESKIMO

PICTURES FROM THE LIFE OF
THE RIGHT REVEREND JOHN HORDEN
FIRST BISHOP OF MOOSONEE

BY

BEATRICE BATTY

GYAN

Published by

Gyan Publishing House
5, Ansari Road
Daryaganj, New Delhi-110002
Phone: 011-47034999, 9811692060
E-mail: books@gyanbooks.com

Distribution Network
gyanbooks.com
India, USA, Canada, UK, Australia, France

ISBN : 978-81-212-3401-6 (PB)
First Published, London, 1893

2nd Impression 2020

Printed at: Gyan Press, Delhi.

Forty-Two Years Amongst the Indians and Eskimo
Author: Beatrice Batty

PREFACE

THE contents of the present volume are in a large measure the outcome of a long-continued personal correspondence with the late Bishop of Moosonee.

As Editor of the *Coral Magazine* I received from him many appeals for aid in the various departments of his work. I asked for graphic descriptions of the surroundings; and I did not ask in vain. Questions concerning the daily life of himself and those about him, the food and habits of the people, modes of travel, dress, climate, products, seasons, and special incidents were duly answered and fully entered into. The bishop had the pen of a ready writer, and all that he wrote was graphic in the extreme. He was, however, modestly unaware of his talent in this respect, until his eyes were opened to the fact by the well-deserved appreciation of the letters and papers which came more frequently and more regularly increasing in interest as time wore on.

The bulk of this book is made up of extracts from this correspondence, with just enough information supplied to give the reader a clear idea of the bishop's life and work. The journal of his first voyage to the distant sphere of his future labours he sent to me in quite recent years, with the expressed hope that it might be published. The various papers and letters afford not only a vivid picture of life amongst the Indians and Eskimo, but a valuable example of what may be accomplished, even under the most untoward circumstances, by indomitable perseverance, unwavering fortitude, and cheerful self-denial, accompanied always by prayer and a firm reliance upon God. 'I can do all things through Christ who strengtheneth me' was the bishop's watch word. His motto—'The happiest man is he who is most diligently employed about his Master's business.'

Should the pictures of life and work offered in the accompanying volume lead others to follow in Bishop Horden's footsteps, their purpose will have been indeed fulfilled.

CONTENTS

A LOG HUT

LIST OF ILLUSTRATIONS

MAP OF MOOSONEE (SCALE, 400 MILES TO THE INCH).

FORTY-TWO YEARS

AMONGST THE

INDIANS AND ESKIMO

CHAPTER I

THE VOYAGE OUT

IN the year 1670, a few English gentlemen, 'the Governor and Company of Adventurers of England trading to Hudson's Bay,' obtained a charter from King Charles II. The company consisted of but nine or ten merchants. They made large profits by bartering English goods with the Indians of those wild, and almost unknown, regions for furs of the fox, otter, beaver, bear, lynx, musk, minx, and ermine.

The company established forts, and garrisoned them with Highlanders and Norwegians. The climate was too cold and the food too coarse to attract Englishmen to the service. The forts, or posts, were about a hundred and fifty or two hundred miles apart, and to them the Indians resorted in the spring of the year with the furs obtained by hunting, snaring, and other modes of capture. In return for these they obtained guns, powder and shot, traps, kettles, axes, cloth, and blankets. The standard of value for everything was a beaver skin. Two white foxes were worth one beaver skin, two silver foxes were worth eight beaver skins, one pocket-handkerchief was worth one beaver skin, one yard of blue cloth was worth one-and-a-half beaver skins, a frying-pan was worth two beaver skins. As time went on, and the value of furs in the market rose or fell, the prices of certain things altered. But this is a sample of what they were when the hero of our tale first went out to Hudson's Bay in 1851.

Let us accompany the young missionary on his voyage to Moose Fort, the chief of the company's trading posts. 'We, that is, my dear wife and myself,' he writes, 'went on board ship at Gravesend on June 6, 1851. Our ship was strongly built, double throughout; it was armed with thick blocks of timber, called ice chocks, at the bows, to enable it to do battle with the ice it would have to encounter. At Stromness we remained a fortnight, taking in a portion of our cargo and a number of men who were going to Hudson's Bay in the service of the company. It was a solitary voyage. All the way we saw but one vessel. On a Saturday afternoon we entered the Straits.

'The weather had been very foggy; but the fog rose, the sun shone out, and a most beautiful spectacle presented itself. The water was as smooth as a fish-pond, and in it were lying blocks of ice of all sizes and shapes, some of them resembling churches, others castles, and others hulls of ships, while at a considerable distance, on either side, rose the wild and dreary land—a land of desolation and death, without a tree or a blade of grass, but high and mountainous, with masses of snow lying in all the hollows. The captain and mates became very anxious. The dangers of the voyage had commenced. An ice-stage, raised eight or nine feet above the deck, was erected, and on this continually walked up and down one or two of the ship's officers. A man, too, was constantly at the bow on the look out, and yet the blows we received were very heavy, setting the bells a-ringing, and causing a sensation of fear.

'When we had got about half-way through the Straits, we saw some of the inhabitants of this dreary land. "The Eskimo are coming," said a sailor.

'By-and-by, I heard the word *Chimo* frequently repeated, which means "Welcome," and presently we saw a number of beautiful little canoes coming towards us, each containing a man. These were soon followed by a large boat containing several women and children. They all came alongside, bringing with them seal-skins, blubber, fox-skins, whalebone, and ivory. These they freely parted with in exchange for pieces of iron, needles, nails, saws, &c., they setting a very great value on anything made of iron. Now these people, who were very, very dirty, were not dressed like English people, but both men and women wore coats made of seal-skins, breeches of dog-skins, and boots of well-dressed seal-skins, the only difference between a man's and a woman's dress being that the woman had a long tail to her coat, reaching almost to the ground, and an immense hood, in which she carried her little naked baby, which was perched on her shoulders.

'Again hoisting our sails, in two or three days we cleared the Straits and entered Hudson's Bay. Danger was not over. Our difficulties had scarcely commenced. Ahead, stretching as far as the eye could reach, is ice—ice; now we are in it. More and more difficult becomes the navigation. We are at a standstill. We go to the mast-head—ice! rugged ice in every direction! One day passes by—two, three, four. The cold is intense. Our hopes sink lower and lower; a week passes. The sailors are allowed to get out and have a game at football; the days pass on; for nearly three weeks we are imprisoned. Then there is a movement in the ice. It is opening. The ship is clear! Every man is on deck. Up with the sails in all speed! Crack, crack, go the blows from the ice through which we are passing; but we shall now soon be free, and in the open sea. Ah! no prisoner ever left his prison with greater joy than we left ours.

'A few days afterwards, as evening was closing in, there was a great commotion on board: heavy chains were got on deck; we were nearing the place of our destination; in the midnight darkness the roar of our guns announced the joyful intelligence that we were anchored at the Second Buoy, only twenty-five miles from Moose Fort.'

Looking at the map of North America, a little inland from the coast of Labrador, you will find Hudson's Bay, and in the south-west corner, at the mouth of the Moose River, Moose Fort. Here is the residence of the deputy governor and his subordinate officers; a number of people are anxiously looking out; they are expecting the one ship that comes to them in the course of the year. A small vessel lying a little way out to sea has raised the long-looked-for signal, and rejoicing is the order of the day.

CHAPTER II

ACQUIRING THE LANGUAGE

OUR travellers were delighted with the appearance of Moose Fort and its immediate surroundings. The little church, the line of neat cottages with their gardens in front, and the new factory buildings, lying irregularly along the banks of the river, gave the place almost the air of an English village. Towering picturesquely above all, was the old fort, strongly built and loopholed, now serving the purpose of a salesroom, but once needed as a place of defence from attacks of the Indians. Poplars, pines, and juniper formed a green background, and the place bore a smiling and pleasant aspect, altogether surprising to those who had expected to arrive on a barren and desolate shore.

Mr. Horden was received with unmistakable joy by the people, who had long been left without a teacher, his predecessor in the office having quitted Moose Fort the year before. He was at once at home amongst the Indians, and immediately set about learning their difficult language.

Greek and Latin he declared to be tame affairs 'in comparison with Sakehao and Ketemakalemão, with their animate and inanimate forms, their direct and inverse, their reciprocal and reflective, their absolute and relative, their want of an infinitive mood, and their two first persons plural. This I found very troublesome for a long time; to use *kelananow* for we, when I meant *I* and *you*; and *nelanan*, when I wished to express *I* and *he*. If merely the extra pronoun had required to be learnt, I should not have minded, but I did mind very much when I found in the verb the pronoun inseparably mixed up with the verb, and that in portions of it the whole of the personal pronouns were expressed by different inflections of the verb. But I had the very strongest of motives to urge me forward: the desire to speak to the Indian in his own language the life-giving words of the Gospel.

'I had been at my new home but a few days before I set to work in earnest. The plan I adopted was this: every week, with the assistance of an interpreter, I translated a small portion of the service of the English Church. This I read over and over again, until I had nearly committed it to memory, and was able to read it on Sunday. The Lord's Prayer and a few hymns I found already translated, and I soon added a few hymns more. Chapters of the Bible and sermons were rendered by the interpreter sentence by sentence. Rather tedious, but we improved fast, and I shall not soon forget the expression of surprise and joy on the countenances of my congregation, when, after a few months, I made my first address to them without an interpreter—but I am anticipating.

'My plan was threefold. I provided myself with two books and a living instructor; the latter a young Indian with a smattering of English. The first of the two books was a small one to carry in my pocket; in it I wrote a few questions with the aid of the interpreter. Having learnt them, I went into an Indian tent, sat down among its inmates, drew out book and pencil, and put one of my questions. One of those present would at once give me an answer, entering generally into a long explanation, of which I did not understand a word. However, they, knowing my aim, talked on, and I listened, wondering what it was all about. Getting gradually bewildered, I returned home. I repeated the process again and again, and after a few days light began to shine out of darkness, the jumble divided itself into words, the book and pencil no longer lay idle, every word that I could separate from the others was at once jotted down, all were copied out, translated as far as possible, and committed to memory; and presently I got not only to catch up the words, but likewise to understand a good deal of what was said.

'The second book was a much larger one, and ruled. Having this and pen and ink by my side, I would call an Indian, and he would take his seat opposite; I then made him understand that I wished him to talk about something, and that I wished to write down what he said. He would begin to speak, but too fast; I shook my head, and said, *Pākack, pākack*—"slowly, slowly," and at a more reasonable rate he would recommence. As he spoke, so I wrote, writing on every other line. We sat thus until I could bear no more. Then, with the interpreter's assistance, I wrote the translation of each word directly under it, thus making an interline. The work was a little trying, but by it I gained words, I gained words in combination, I gained the inflections of words, I gained the idiom of the language, I gained a knowledge of the mind of the Indian, the channel in which his ideas ran, I gained a knowledge of his mode of life, the trials and privations to which he was subjected.

'Now as to the Indian lad. I began by drilling him in the powers of an English verb, and after a few days we said a lesson to each other, he saying—First person singular, I love; second person singular, thou lovest, &c. Then I going on with mine. thus:

Ne sakehou . . .	I love him.
Ke sakehou . . .	Thou lovest him.
Sakehao . . .	He loves him.
Ne sakehanam . .	We love him.
Ke sakehanou . .	We love him.
Ke sakehawou . .	You love him.
Sakehawuh . .	They love him.

Then the inverse form:

Ne sakehik . . .	Me loves he.
Ke sakehik . . .	Thee loves he.
Sakehiko . . .	He is loved by him.
Ne sakihikonau . .	Us loves he.
Ke sakehikonau . .	Us loves he.
Ke sakehikowou . .	You loves he.
Sakehikowuk . .	They are loved by him.

And so on and on. The subjunctive mood, with its *iks* and *uks* and *aks* and *chucks*, was terribly formidable, still the march was onward, every week the drudgery became less and the pleasure greater, and every week I was able to enter more and more into conversation with those who formed my spiritual charge.

'In my talk I made mistakes enough. Once I had a class of young men sitting around me, and was telling them of the creation of Adam and Eve. All went well until I came to speak of Eve's creation ; I got as far as "God created Eve out of one of Adam's ——," when something more than a smile broke forth from my companions. Instead of saying, "out of one of Adam's ribs," I had said, "out of one of Adam's pipes." *Ospikakun* is "his rib," and *ospwakun*, "his pipe."

'After eight months I never used an interpreter in my public ministrations, and I had been in the country but a few days more than a twelvemonth, when, standing by the side of good Bishop Anderson, I interpreted his sermon to a congregation of Albany Indians. I say this with deep thankfulness to God for assisting me in my formidable undertaking.'

CHAPTER III

EARLY LIFE

MR. HORDEN had not only a wonderful power of acquiring languages, but a wonderful power of adapting himself to all things, people, and circumstances. This stood him in good stead throughout his career. Born in Exeter, January 20, 1828, in humble circumstances, simply educated, apprenticed to a trade in early boyhood, he lived to attain a high position. All difficulties were overcome by his dauntless energy of purpose and unwavering perseverance.

He wished to study, but his father put him to a smithy. He desired to become a missionary, but his relatives discouraged the idea. He did not rebel, he did not kick against authority, but he neglected no opportunity to further his purpose. He read and thought, he attended evening Bible readings, he taught in the Sunday school, and when his indentures were out he left the anvil for the desk. He obtained the post of usher in a boys' school. And now being independent, he offered himself to the Church Missionary Society, with a view to going to India as a lay agent, and he was accepted with the understanding that he would await a suitable opening, which might perhaps not occur for two or three years.

He was willing to wait, but his patience was not to be tried. The society learnt that the Wesleyans had withdrawn from Hudson's Bay, and that there was great need of a teacher at Moose Fort. Here was an opening for a young man such as John Horden appeared to be. Hastily he was telegraphed for—Hudson's Bay was not India! But he was willing to go. It were better he should take a wife with him. The lady was ready, like-minded with himself. They must start in three weeks. They agreed to do it. He went home, got married, and returned to London. The needful outfit was hastily prepared, and they started, as we have seen. Such in short is the story of our hero's earlier life.

Large and varied were to be his experiences in his later years. The society at home hearing of his success with the Indians, his great progress in learning the language, and his ready adaptability to all the requirements of the post, had determined to send him to the Bishop of Rupert's Land for ordination. 'But,' said the bishop, 'this plan was formed in ignorance of the distance and difficulties of travelling in this part of the country, and I did not wish to expose Mr. Horden with wife and baby to it.' Bishop Anderson chose rather to traverse his huge diocese and ordain the young missionary at Moose.

On the morning of June 28, in the year 1852, the start was made from St. Andrews, Red River, in a canoe decorated by one of the bishop's scholars with a mitre and the Union flag at the stern, and at the bow a rose and duck. For the latter 'I might have substituted the dove with the olive branch, had I known of it in time,' says the bishop, 'but it was done to surprise me, and the more familiar object was naturally enough selected.' The provisions consisted largely of flour and pemmican, the clothing, of the bishop's robes and a few necessaries, the bedding, of a pillow with a buffalo robe and blankets. The journey lasted six weeks. Throughout it the bishop confirmed, married, and baptized as he passed from post to post, and on arriving at Moose Fort the work was repeated. He found the Indians full of love and regard for their teacher. 'He has their hearts and affections,' he wrote, 'and their eyes turn to him at once. This is his best testimonial for holy orders.'

Careful examination of the candidate still further convinced the bishop of his suitability, and when the annual ship arrived bringing an English clergyman, the Rev. E. A. Watkins, destined for Fort George, he no longer delayed, but ordained Mr. Horden both deacon and priest, Mr. Watkins presenting. The bishop and Mr. Watkins had then to hasten on their several ways, lest early winter might overtake them ere they reached their destinations. And so the ardent, earnest young catechist was left at Moose, pastor as well as teacher of his flock, known to and esteemed by every man, woman and child of the Indian families who resorted thither during the summer season, and supremely happy in his work and position.

The home in which he and his wife dwelt was of the simplest, its walls were of plain pine wood; but within it was enlivened by the baby prattle of their first-born child, baptized by the bishop, Elizabeth Anderson. Without, it was surrounded by a garden, in which some hardy flowers grew side by side with potatoes, turnips, peas, and barley. Moose is not by any means bare of wild flowers, and in mosses it is very rich, whilst goodly clumps of trees waved their branches in the breeze on an island only five minutes' walk from the house. During the winter the missionary and his family, together with the three or four gentlemen of the Hudson's Bay Company, with their servants, and a few sick and aged Indians and children, were the sole inhabitants of the settlement. Then Mr. Horden gave himself up to his little school, to his translation work, and to such building operations as in course of time became necessary—a school-house, a church, a new dwelling-house. After dinner he was occupied with hammer, chisel, saw and plane until dark. In the evening he gave instruction to a few young men.

One such, whom he employed for a time as a school assistant in later years, he had the pleasure of sending in due course for ordination by the Bishop of Rupert's Land, who appointed him to the charge of Albany station, one hundred miles north of Moose, an important outpost, at which eighty families of Indians congregated during the summer. Hannah Bay, another post, fifty miles east of Moose, was resorted to by fifty families; Rupert's House, one hundred miles east, was frequented by sixty families; and Kevoogoonisse, 430 miles south, by thirty families. All these places were to be visited by Mr. Horden, as well as Martin's Falls, three hundred miles from Albany, and Osnaburg, two hundred miles further on; also Flying Post, one hundred from Kevoogoonisse, and New Brunswick, one hundred from Flying Post.

This was sufficient to appal the mind and daunt the courage of one still young and inexperienced. It did not daunt John Horden. He longed only to teach all who were thus placed under his ministerial charge. The journeys must be made at particular seasons, as throughout the greater part of the year no Indians were at the trading-posts.

CHAPTER IV

WINTER AT MOOSE FORT

THE four seasons are called in the Indian tongue, Sekwun, Nepin, Tukwaukin, and Pepooa. Spring begins about the middle or end of May, when the ice in the river breaks up. Vegetation proceeds rapidly. In a few days the bushes look green, and within a fortnight the grass and trees appear in summer garb. Sometimes the 'breaking-up' is attended with danger, often with inconvenience.

In the spring of 1860 the little settlement was visited with a disastrous flood. The ground all around is low, not a hill within seventy miles. Mr. Horden was occupied in building his new church—the frame already rested on the foundations. One Sunday morning it floated off and took an excursion of nearly a quarter of a mile, and with the aid of ropes, poles, and other implements it had to be dragged back to its former position and strongly secured. 'The ice,' said Mr. Horden, 'made much more havoc than it did in '57. A few days after the water had subsided I found my garden thickly planted with ice blocks of a considerable size; but our gardening operations were not impeded, we were able to raise a large quantity of potatoes of very good quality. The effects of a flood are not always evident at once; it is after the lapse of months that they become apparent, when the poor Indian on arriving at his winter hunting-grounds finds that the water has been there, and destroyed nearly the whole of the rabbits. He is reduced to great straits, and the energies of the whole family are required to keep them from starvation.'

Rabbits are the staple food of the Indians in the season. The skins, being of little value for barter, are used by them as blankets, the women sewing them very neatly together.

In 1861 Mr. Horden writes: 'In May we were again threatened with a flood. On returning from church one Sunday evening the river presented an awful appearance. The strength of the current had broken up the ice, and formed it into a conical shape, which rose as high as the tops of the trees on the high bank of the river. We abandoned our house, having first taken every precaution to guard against the fury of the waters, but, although the threat was so formidable, we experienced no flood, and after spending a few pleasant days at the establishment of the Hudson's Bay Company we returned, and at once began our gardening. The children look upon a flood as a rare treat. To them it is something of a pleasant, exciting nature, after the dull monotony of a seven or eight months' winter. It drives us from our house, but we take shelter in one equally good, where we ourselves enjoy pleasant company, and where the children have a large number of playmates. What we look upon as our greatest trial are the privations and sufferings to which the Indians are subjected.'

Nepin is very changeable, sometimes excessively warm, with plenty of mosquitoes and sand-flies, which are very troublesome; sometimes quite cold, and the transition is very rapid. It may be hot in the morning, and in the evening so cold that an overcoat may be worn with comfort.

'This is the busy season,' writes Mr. Horden, 'when I take my journeys. Brigades of canoes from the various posts arrive, bringing the furs collected during the preceding winter; in fact, every person appears to have plenty to do.' Just as summer is ending, the ship arrives, and it is very anxiously looked for, for on it almost everything depends—flour, tea, clothing, books, everything.

'Tukwaukin is generally very boisterous, with occasional hail and snow storms. Then the Indians hunt geese, which are salted and put into barrels for our use, although they are not quite so good as a corned round of beef. Before the arrival of Pepooa, all of the Indians are gone off to their winter grounds, from which most of them do not return until the arrival of spring.'

Each point of Mr. Horden's vast parish had to be reached by an arduous journey. Arduous is indeed but a mild expression for the troubles, trials, privations, and tremendous difficulties attendant on travel through the immense, trackless wastes lying between many of the posts—wastes intersected with rivers and rapids, varied only by tracts of pathless forest, swept by severe storms. 'Last autumn,' he writes, 'I took a journey to Kevoogoonisse; it is 430 miles distant, and during the whole way I saw no tent or house, not even a human being, until I arrived within a short distance of the post. I appeared to be passing through a forgotten land; I saw trees by tens of thousands, living, decaying, and dead; I saw majestic waterfalls, and passed through fearful rapids; I walked over long and difficult places, and day after day struck my little tent, and felt grieved at seeing no new faces, none to whom I might impart some spiritual blessing. In the whole space of country over which I travelled, perhaps a dozen Indian families hunt during the winter. Sometimes even this tract is insufficient to supply their wants; animals become scarce, the lands are burnt by the forest fires, and they are reduced to the greatest distress. I have seen terrible cases of this kind. I have seen a man with an emaciated countenance, who in one winter lost six children, all he had; and, horrible to relate, nearly every one of them was killed for the purpose of satisfying the cravings of hunger. At the post to which he was attached, Kevoogoonisse, out of about 120 Indians, twenty died through starvation in one winter.'

The country may be said to be one vast forest, with very extensive plains, watered by large rivers and numerous lakes, inhabited by a few roving Indians, who are engaged in hunting wild animals to procure furs for the use of civilized man.

Sometimes sad things took place during the absence of the missionary on his journeyings to visit outlying stations. During the short summer of 1858, he set out with his wife and their little children to visit Whale River, in the country of the Eskimo. It was not his first journey to that post. 'You will have need of all your courage,' said he to his wife. Tempestuous seas, shelterless nights, and stormy days were vivid to his own memory, but wife and children were glad to see anything new, after the monotonous days and nights of the long Moose winter.

The family had not long been gone, when whooping-cough broke out at Moose. Young, old, and middle-aged were attacked alike, and numbers died. So terrible was the sickness that at one time there was but one man able to work, and his work was to make two coffins. The missionary returned to a sorrowing people. Out of five European families four had lost each a child, and 'the sight of the grave-yard and the mothers weeping there is one I never shall forget. In ordinary years the average mortality was two. This year it was thirty-two.' Amongst the children taken was dear little Susan, the orphan child of a heathen Indian, whom they had cared for from infancy, and whose little fingers had just before her illness traced upon a sampler the text: 'Remember now thy Creator in the days of thy youth, while the evil days' —— Here the words had ceased—she was taken from all evil, and the evil days would not draw nigh her, the needle remained in the sampler at that spot. Amongst the aged taken were blind Koote, old blind Adam, and old blind Hannah, all of whom are specially mentioned in Mr. Horden's account of the previous Christmas Day services.

'Yesterday,' he writes, speaking of Christmas 1857, 'was a deeply interesting one to me. As usual, I met the Indians at seven, the English-speaking congregation at eleven, and Indians again at three. Among the communicants present were no less than three blind persons. Old Adam, over whose head have, I should think, passed a hundred winters. Old Koote, always at church, led with a string by a little boy, and poor old lame Hannah, whose seat is seldom empty, be the weather what it may. The day previous to our communion we had a meeting of the communicants. Old blind Koote said, "I thank God for having preserved me to this day. God is good! I pray to Him every night and morning. That does good to my soul. I think a great deal about heaven, I ask Jesus to wash away all my sins, and to take me there."'

Any of the Indians who can come in to celebrate the Christmas and New Year's festivals eagerly seize the opportunity. But this is not possible for the greater number, whose hunting-grounds lie at considerable distances from the fort. In their far-away tents they have no means of Christian communion or instruction, except by intercourse with one another, and by the study of the portions of Scripture, prayers, and hymns which they gladly and thankfully carry away with them to their lonely homes in the wilderness.

The society had sent out a printing-press to Moose Fort, to facilitate the supply of books to the Indians. Mr. Horden had hoped to receive by the ship copies of his translations ready printed, instead of which, to his dismay, blank sheets arrived with the press. He was no printer, although his father had been, and now his energy, courage, and power to overcome difficulties pre-eminently showed themselves. He shut himself up in his room for several days, resolved to master the putting together of the press ; a very complicated business. But he accomplished it, and great was his joy and triumph when he found that the machinery would work. From this press issued, in one winter, no less than sixteen hundred books in three Indian dialects.

The winter over and gone, the snow nearly disappeared, day after day the geese and wavies are seen flying overhead. The mighty river, which has been for many months locked up, with a giant's strength has burst its bonds asunder, and rushes impetuously towards the sea ; a few birds appear in the trees. the frogs have commenced their croaking, fish find their way to the well-laid nets ; and the busy mosquito has begun its unwelcome buzz. The Indians collect their furs, tie them in bundles, and place them in the canoes, and with their dogs and household stuff they make their way down stream to the trader's residence. They run a few rapids, carry their canoe and baggage over many portages, sail the frail bark over one or two lakes, and are at the end of their journey. Down come the

A TRADER'S STORE

trader's servants to help to carry the packs to the store.

Let us look around. The store contains everything that an Indian needs, whether for business or comfort. Here a rack full of guns, there a pile of thick blankets, a bale of blanket coats, and an almost unlimited supply of blue and red cloth ; axes and knives, matches and kettles, beads and braid, deer-skin and moose-skin, powder and shot, twine for nets and snares, tea and sugar, flour and oatmeal, pork and pease ; and some good books too, which tell the Indian of God and heaven, and which he can read.

The trader approaches, his face beaming with delight as he eyes the packs, for they are large and valuable. He soon begins work. The first bale contains nothing but beaver skins. Eighty-five examined are said to be worth a hundred and twenty beaver according to the standard value. The next contains forty marten, ten otter, a hundred and fifty rat. These are adjudged worth a hundred beaver ; the third bale is composed of five hundred rabbit skins, worth twenty-five beaver. Consider a beaver equal to two shillings and sixpence, and you will see the value of the hunt in sterling money. We have now—bale one value one hundred and twenty beaver ; bale two value one hundred beaver ; and bale three value twenty-five beaver ; altogether two-hundred-and-forty-five beaver. Last summer yonder Indian took out a debt in goods of one hundred and fifty beaver, this he pays, and then he has ninety-five beaver with which to trade. Ninety-five quills are given to him, and his trading begins. The trader, like an English shopman, stands behind a counter, and the Indian outside. Native-like, he consults long before the purchase of each article. Having decided, he calls out, 'A gun;' a gun is delivered, and he pays over ten of his quills; then three yards of cloth, for which he pays two quills; two books, and for them he pays one quill; and so on he goes, the heap of goods increasing and the supply of quills decreasing gradually. As he approaches the end, the consultation becomes very anxious; he is making quite sure that he is laying out his money to the best advantage. But the end comes at last, and, satisfied with his bargains, he gathers all up into one of the purchased blankets, and retires to his tent, where he examines and admires, and admires again, article after article.

Shall we take a peep into an Indian's tent when encamped in the forest on a trapping expedition? A fire burns in the centre, but through the large opening overhead we see the snow lying thick on the branches of the trees. The day has just broken, but the Christian Indian has already engaged in worship and taken his morning meal. Then on with his snow-shoes, for there is no moving without them. The blanket which forms the tent door is raised, and he steps outside. How cold! and how drear the scene! how still and death-like! no birds, no sound, save the wind whistling through the forest. Now he is at a marten trap, a very simple contrivance, composed of a framework of sticks, in the middle of which a bait is placed, which being meddled with, causes the descent of a log, which crushes the intruder. Here is a beautiful dark marten, quite a prize. He takes it out and fastens it to a sledge, re-baits the trap, and on he goes to another. Ah! he sees tracks, but the marten has not entered the trap; on to another. What is this? He looks dismayed; a wolverine has been here, and has robbed the trap. He resets it and goes on to the next; the wolverine has been there too; to another and another, with the same result. He is disheartened, but it cannot be helped. So he trudges on over a round of thirty traps, taking altogether six fine martens; not a bad day's hunt, all things considered. Evening is drawing on. He returns to the tent, and there awaits him a glorious repast, perhaps of beaver meat. He feels quite refreshed, and recounts all the vicissitudes of the day, the gains and disappointments.

On the morrow he takes the martens and skins them; and what is he to do with the bodies? Our Indian friends are not fastidious. He eats them. The skins he turns inside out, and stitches them up. In the spring he brings them to the fur-trading post, and there exchanges them, as we have seen, for all the requisites of Indian life. An Indian cannot afford to cast away anything; all he kills is to him 'beef,' sometimes good, sometimes not a little bad. 'In my own experience,' Mr. Horden says, 'I have eaten white bear, black bear, wild cat, while for a week or ten days together I have had nothing but beaver, and glad indeed I have been to get it.'

When the Indians have come into the post the work of instruction at once commences. Amid school-work, services, visiting and talking with individuals, the missionary found his time fully occupied. Little leisure remained for his dearly-loved translation work —yet this progressed. In 1859 Mr. Horden had already the prayer and hymn book and the four Gospels printed in the syllabic character. The prayer and hymn book were printed in England. The Gospels he had himself printed at Moose. 'The performance of this labour,' he writes, 'was almost too much for me, as, since last winter, although not incapacitated for work, I have felt that even a very strong constitution has limits, which it may not pass with impunity; I have occasionally suffered from weakness of the chest. I need not say with what delight the Indians received the books prepared for them. I did not think it right to provide them all gratis, I therefore charged two shillings each, a little less than one beaver skin, and with the money thus raised I am able to purchase a year's consumption of paper. Our services are now conducted in a manner very similar to what they are at home. Our meetings for prayer are extremely refreshing, and my spirit is often revived by joining with my brethern around the throne of grace.'

It must be remembered that Mr. Horden had not only the Indians under his ministry, but the Europeans of the Hudson's Bay Company; thus he had English as well as Indian services to hold, and as there were some Norwegians amongst the company's servants who did not readily follow either the English or the Indian, he set himself to learn for their sake sufficient Norwegian to read the service and to preach to them in their own tongue.

To these languages he added Eskimo and Ojibbeway—the latter being the speech of the people of the Kevoogoonisse district, the former that of the natives of Whale River.

How could all this be crowded into the busy day of this father of his flock? How but by rising in the small hours of the morning, when by the light of a lamp in his little study he read, and wrote, and translated, and in addition to all else taught himself Hebrew.

CHAPTER V

A VISIT TO THE ESKIMO AT WHALE RIVER

IN February 1861, Mr. Horden writes, 'My hands are quite full ; I find it impossible to do all that I should wish to do. On Sundays I hold three full services, and attend school twice, and every morning except Saturday I conduct school. On Tuesday afternoon and Wednesday evening I hold a service. These matters, with my house and sick visiting, leave me very little leisure. But as myself and my family enjoy good health, I can say that happiness is to be found as well among the primeval forests of Moosonee as in the more sunny land of our birth.'

For his Eskimo children the bishop always had a very special affection. Very early in his missionary career he managed, as we have seen, to pay them a visit. He then could not converse with them, nor could he do so without the aid of an interpreter when he paid a summer visit to Whale River about the year 1862. We give his own graphic account of this.

'Let our thoughts for a while be transferred to a land more bleak and desolate than Moose, to the land where snow never entirely disappears, to the land of barren rock and howling storm, to the country of the white bear and the hardy Eskimo, where I spent some time last summer. I remained with the Eskimo only eight days, yet those eight days were indeed blessed ones, and will not soon be forgotten by me, for they were amongst the most successful missionary days I have had since I have been in the country.

'The Eskimo appeared to me to be kind, cheerful, docile, persevering, and honest. Nothing could exceed the desire they professed for instruction, nothing the exertions they made to learn to read, nothing the attention with which they listened to the Word of God. I was most fortunate (but should I not use another word?) in obtaining the services of a young Eskimo as my interpreter, who had received instruction from missionaries (Moravians) while living on the coast of Labrador. He spoke English but imperfectly; but knew some hymns and texts exceedingly well, and showed himself most willing to assist me to the fullest extent of his power. I could not have done half the work I did, had I not had him as my assistant. Accompany me for a day, commencing with the early morning.

'Soon after six we had a service with the Eskimo; about twenty-five were present. Some of the men were dressed very much like working men in England. They purchase their clothing from the store of the Hudson's Bay Company. Others were dressed in the comfortable native style, composed of a loose seal-skin jacket coming to the waist, seal-skin breeches, and seal-skin boots. One of the women had on an English gown, of which she seemed not a little proud; the others were attired in a dress somewhat similar to the men, with the addition of an immense hood to their jackets, in which they deposit their little babies.

'The service was commenced by singing a hymn; reading followed, then prayer, the Lord's Prayer being repeated aloud by all; singing again; then a long lesson on the "Syllabariam," *i.e.* the system of reading by syllables, without the labour of spelling. They were then instructed in Watt's First Catechism, and another hymn completed the service. After having taken my breakfast, I assembled the Indians, who were nearly twice the number of the Eskimo, but not half as painstaking. My service with them was somewhat less simple than that with the Eskimo, as they had received more instruction, and a few could use their prayer books intelligently; but I noticed an apathy among them which rather disheartened me.

'I then took a lesson from my Eskimo interpreter, writing questions and obtaining his assistance in translating a portion of the baptismal and marriage services; I then went to the Eskimo tents until dinner-time. They are made of seal-skins in the shape of a common marquee. Some of them are spacious and not very dirty. In the centre is a fire, over which is suspended a large kettle full of cray-fish. An old woman was sewing very industriously at a pair of seal-skin short boots, which she presented to me. Her husband was equally industrious, making models of Eskimo implements. I instantly trans-

A GROUP OF ESKIMO

ferred to paper the few words of conversation they had with me. My next visit was to a tent where younger people were assembled. I asked a few questions, which they readily answered. I was pleased at this, as showing that they could understand me. I then dined, and took a short stroll along the river towards the sea, to see what prospect there was for the whale fishermen. The fishers were there, waiting patiently, but with the look of disappointment on their countenances. They could see hundreds of whales outside the bar of the river, but while they remained there not one could be caught, and there seemed no chance of any coming inside the bar. Leaving them, I went to hold a second service with my Eskimo, then another with my Indians. It was then tea-time. I spent an hour with my Eskimo interpreter, after which I held an English service with the master and mistress, the only English-speaking woman for hundreds of miles, and the European servants of the company. Half an hour's social chat at length closed the day, and with feelings of thankfulness at having been placed as a labourer in the vineyard of the Lord, I retired to rest.

'I was so deeply impressed with the conduct of the Eskimo, their anxiety to learn, and their love for the truths of Christianity, that I could not forbid water that some of them should be baptized. Three of them could read well; these received the rite of baptism at an evening service, all the Europeans being present, for all appeared to take a deep interest in the proceedings. All three were young, neat, tidy, and dressed in European costume. They answered my inquiries very intelligently, receiving severally the names of John Horden, Thomas Henry, and Elizabeth Oke. John and Elizabeth were afterwards married. Malikto, the father of the bridegroom, stood up at the conclusion of the service, and said that he hoped they would not . ·get the instruction they had received, after I left them. It was a delightful but solemn service.'

The Eskimo formed a large part of Mr. Horden's charge, and he was much attracted by their gentle contentment amidst their dreary surroundings, and by their teachableness. 'What should we have been, had we, like them,' he said, 'had no Bible to direct us to God?'

Thus speaks the Eskimo, the man who considers himself pre-eminently the 'man,' and who has *not* been taught that God made him, the sun, and the moon, and the stars also:

'Long, long ago, not long after the creation of the world, there lived a mighty Eskimo, who was a great conjurer; nothing was impossible to him; no other of his profession could stand before him. He found the world too small and insignificant for his powers, so, taking with him his sister and a small fire, he raised himself up into the heavens. Heaping immense quantities of fuel on the fire, he formed the sun, which has continued burning ever since. For a while he and his sister lived together in perfect harmony, but after a time he began to ill-treat her, and his conduct towards her became worse and worse until one day he scorched her face, which was exquisitely beautiful. This was not to be borne, she therefore fled from him, and formed the moon. Her brother is still in chase of her, but although he sometimes gets near her, he will never overtake her. When it is new moon the burnt side of her face is towards us ; when full moon the reverse is the case. The stars are the spirits of the dead Eskimo that have fixed themselves in the heavens, and meteors and the aurora are these spirits moving from one place to another whilst visiting their friends.'

CHAPTER VI

SCHOOL WORK

In school work and teaching Mr. Horden took from first to last the keenest interest. After he became bishop he still visited the Moose School daily, whenever he was in residence. In earlier years he had for a time the able assistance of a native master, Mr. Vincent. A small boarding-school had been commenced in 1855 with two children, who were supported through the Coral Missionary Fund.[1] The following year, two more children were taken, and in 1857 the number on the list amounted to eight; to these others were yearly added, supported by friends of the Coral Fund.

Little Susan was one of these. Her unfinished sampler with the needle in it was sent to England. The children's histories were many of them very sad and pathetic. Some were orphans. The parents of others were disabled, or too sick and suffering to work. One little girl was described as having so wild a look that a portrait of her scarcely resembled that of a

[1] At the instance of the then editors of the *Coral Missionary Magazine.*

human being. Another, after remaining for a time in the school, fell ill with the strange Indian sickness called 'long thinking,' a gypsy-like yearning for the wild life of the forest, and she had to be sent back to her widowed father. One boy died early of decline, a complaint to which the Indian is very subject. Another was the child of a father who lay sick and bed-ridden in a most deplorable condition—parts of his body actually rotten. 'He might have been the Lazarus of the parable,' wrote Mr. Horden. 'He gets little rest night or day, but, like Lazarus, his mind is stayed on God.'

A few children having thus been gathered together with the certainty of support, Mr. Horden commenced building a school-house. He had from the first assembled the children for daily instruction, but to board and clothe them was impossible without some friendly help, all necessaries at Moose being nearly double the price of the same articles at home. At one time it was quite double. From this we may gather with what delight was hailed, as the season came round, the arrival of the annual ship, bringing to the missionary and his family the stores needed for themselves and their charges for the year to come.

In 1864 very especially, Mr. and Mrs. Horden awaited in eager expectation the ship's appearance, for not only did they long to know that the wants of the school children and the poor who depended upon them would be supplied, but they were hoping themselves to return in her with their little family for a well-earned rest and change in England, from which country they had then been absent thirteen long years. The three elder children were of an age to need an English education. The little son, a boy of nine or ten, whose principal amusement was to go to the woods with an axe over his shoulder to cut fire-wood, must, ere it was too late, be weaned from the free life in the forest, and begin to measure his powers of mind and body with other lads of his age and class at home. The wife and mother yearned to see the relatives parted from long ago; the hard-worked man hoped for stimulus and help in the society and sympathy of his brethren and fellow-labourers.

These hopes and yearnings were doomed to disappointment. 'You know,' wrote Mr. Horden on January 25, 1865, 'that it was my intention to be at home this year, and I had expected to have reached England in October or the beginning of November. But August passed and the ship did not arrive, and anxiety increased daily. The 23rd came, the latest day on which the ship had ever been known to appear, and then we began to despond and to say, "No ship this year!" The schooner still remained outside, hoping against hope, until October 7. That same night, in the midst of a most fearful storm, we heard the report of large guns at sea; our excitement was extreme, our hopes revived, and from mouth to mouth passed the joyful exclamation, "The ship's come! the ship's come!" We lay down to rest, lightened of a great weight of anxiety, dreaming of absent friends, with a strange pleasant confusion of boxes, storms, ice, guns, and the many other etceteras of the sailing, arrival, and unloading of our ship.

'Morning dawned, the storm had subsided, a boat was despatched for letters, the schooner was again ordered to sea, all hearts beat high, and by ten o'clock our illusions were dispelled. The guns had been fired by the York schooner, which had been despatched to Moose to acquaint us with our misfortune, and to bring the little that had been saved from the wreck. It was very little, yet sufficient to remove anxiety as to our living for this winter, as we thus became possessed of flour and tea, which we can only obtain by the ship, for in our wintry land no fields of wheat wave their golden heads, and no sound of the reapers ever falls upon the ear. Of the many packages sent me, the Coral Fund box was the only one which came to hand, all the rest are at the bottom of the sea: and of the contents of your box, everything was much damaged, except the service book, now lying on the communion table at Moose. The packet-box was saved, which accounts for my receiving your letter.

'The Moose ship left England in company with the Hudson's Bay Company's ship, bound for York Factory, which is a post about seven hundred miles north of Moose, and came across the Atlantic and nearly through Hudson's Straits without any mishaps. On August 13 the two ships were together, a few miles to the east of Mansfield Island; the captains visited and congratulated each other upon having passed the most dangerous portion of the voyage, and expected that within a week the one would be at York and the other at Moose. But how blind is man! Within a few hours both of them were ashore on Mansfield Island, about twelve miles distant from each other. The York ship had a very large number of men on board, and by almost incredible exertions she was got off, but not until she had sustained such damages as necessitated the constant use of the pumps. The Moose ship could not be got off, and still lies with nearly all her valuable cargo on the rocks. The York ship came to her and took all the crew on board, together with what had been saved, and proceeded to York Factory. There she was examined, and then it appeared how near all had been to death; the wonder was how she could possibly have kept afloat. To return to England in her would have been madness, so she still lies at York. Happily a second vessel had gone to York, which took home nearly the whole of the crews of the two disabled ships.

'When I last wrote I asked for the service book for my new church; that edifice has now, I am happy to say, been opened; the interesting ceremony took place on Whit-Sunday, May 15, 1864. The ice had entirely disappeared from the river; the sun shone forth brilliantly, all Nature smiled. A large congregation assembled at our usual hour for service, and all seemed impressed with the solemnity of the occasion. The subject of the sermon was the dedication of Solomon's temple. At its close the collection amounted to upwards of 4*l*., and after that a number of Europeans, natives, and Indians, assembled round the table of the Lord. It was the first time I ever administered a general communion, many of the Indians not understanding English; but on this occasion I wished them to see that, in spite of diversity of language, God is alike the God of the white man and the red. Altogether it was a most interesting and happy day. It is literally a church in the wilderness. I hope it will not be long before others rise in this part of the country.

'I have lately heard of my poor Eskimo brethren in the far-off desert; that infant church has been much tried. Just one half of its members have been carried off by death; there were but four, two of whom are gone, and both somewhat suddenly. One of them was the young Eskimo interpreter, who when I was last with them was of such very great service to me. Late in the fall he went off in his kayak to set a fox trap. He did so, but as he was getting into the canoe to return home it upset with him, and the coldness of the water prevented him from swimming. His body was not discovered until the evening of the following day. The other was the only baptized woman, her name was Elizabeth Horden. These trials must be necessary, or they would not be sent.'

CHAPTER VII

FIRST RETURN TO ENGLAND

In 1865 Mr. Horden and his family came home; the journey was a long and very anxious one. 'Among the many dangerous voyages which our bold sailors undertake,' he writes, 'there is none more dangerous, or attended with more anxiety, than the one to or from Moose Factory. Hudson's Straits are dangerous, Hudson's Bay fearfully so, James's Bay worst of all. It is full of sunken rocks and shoals; it is noted for its fogs.

'When the ship came, it was in a somewhat disabled condition, so severely had she been handled by the ice. However, we repaired her at Moose, and although it was very late in the season we determined, putting ourselves in God's hands, to trust ourselves in her. We left Moose with a fair wind, which took us in safety over our long, crooked, and dangerous bar; but we had not proceeded above half a day's sail before a heavy storm came upon us. Dangers were around us, the dread of all coming to Moose Factory, the Gasket Shoal, was ahead; the charts were frequently consulted; the captain was anxious, sleep departed from his eyes. We are at the commencement of the straits ; we see land, high, rugged, barren hills ; snow is lying in the valleys, stern winter is already come ; it seems a home scarcely fit for the white bear and the walrus. What are these solitary giants, raising their heads so high, and appearing so formidable ? They are immense icebergs which have come from regions still farther north, and are now being carried by the current through Hudson's Straits into the Atlantic Ocean. The glass speaks of coming bad weather, the top-sails are reefed, reefs are put to the main-sail ; and now it is on us, the wind roars through the rigging, the ship plunges and creaks. Night comes over the scene, there is no cessation of the tempest ; it howls and roars, it is a fearful night! One of the boats is nearly swept away, and is saved with difficulty ; we have lost some of our rigging ; one man is washed overboard, and washed back again. The sea breaks over the vessel, and dashes into the cabin ; but One mightier has said, "Hitherto shalt thou come, and no farther." By the morning, the morning of the Sabbath, the wind had abated.'

Dreary weeks followed ; the time for arrival in England had long since passed, and our travellers were still beating about in the Atlantic. Luxuries had vanished, comforts had departed, necessaries were becoming very scarce, and they began to ask each other, 'Is England ever to be reached ?' Then the children saw a steamer for the first time in their lives, and their surprise was great ; and now they pass vessel after vessel. They are running up the English Channel, a pilot comes on board, and on they go, till they are safely moored in the West India Docks. Now to a railway station and into a railway carriage, out of that and into a cab through the busiest part of London ; the shops are brilliantly lighted up ; the children are at the windows, their exclamations of surprise are incessant, a new world is opened to their view—a world of bustle, a world of life.

Mr. Horden spent a busy year in England, travelling, as he expressed it, 'from Dan to Beersheba,' speaking on behalf of 'his beloved people' and his work ; everywhere eliciting sympathy and interest In his absence from the station Mr. Vincent of Albany had gone to Moose, to provide for the spiritual wants of the flock and to keep the school going. The children were examined before the Christmas holidays in Scripture and Catechism and arithmetic, after which they were rewarded with little presents sent in the bales from England. He reported the mission as presenting a cheering aspect. 'From every quarter,' he writes, 'the heathen are being gradually brought under the influence of the Gospel ; we have much cause for encouragement, but we also meet with opposition. I visited an outpost in the Rupert's River district last summer, about five hundred and fifty miles distant from this station, called Mistasinnee. Both there and on the way I had frequent opportunities of preaching the Gospel to anxious inquirers, and before leaving that post I had forty-eight baptisms, half the number being adults ; the trip occupied about two months. We are having a very mild winter, but not a favourable one for living, as rabbits and partridges are very scarce. Sometimes we have a difficulty in making up something for dinner. I hope, however, as the season advances, we shall do better, for partridges then will be returning to the northward, and we may get a few in passing.'

CHAPTER VIII

AGAIN AT WORK

AT the end of the year Mr. Horden returned to Moose with his wife and two youngest children, and that same year the homeward-bound ship was once more in imminent peril. And now our hero began a series of long journeys, the longest he had made —one occupying three months and covering nearly two thousand miles — amongst people of various languages. He thus vividly describes it:

'I left Moose Factory for Brunswick House in the afternoon of May 20, 1868. The weather was very cold, and on the following morning we left our encampment amidst a fall of snow. All along the river banks the ice lay piled up in heaps, occasionally forming a wall twenty feet high. This ice was very detrimental to our progress; it prevented the Indians from tracking the canoe, so that they were forced to use the paddle or pole, which is harder work and does not permit of such rapid progress. We got on pretty well until we came to where the river rushes with awful rapidity between high and almost perpendicular rocks: it certainly appeared like travelling to destruction. We had to cross the river several times, so as to get where the current was weakest. We had crossed twice, and bad enough it was each time; we were to cross the third time; our guide demurred. It could not be done with safety; we should be driven down a foaming rapid and destroyed.

'But it was now just as dangerous to go backward as forward, so, after a little persuading, the old man was induced to try. I took a paddle, and we got out into the middle of the stream, paddling for our lives; we were carried a considerable way down, but the other side was reached in safety. Then we poled, or tracked, on, as we best could, very slowly, until we had to cross again, and so on until the first portage was reached. Over this we plod, and again our canoe floats into the river; then pole, paddle, or track until a majestic fall or a roaring rapid warned us to make another portage; and so on, again and again, day after day.

'As we went towards the south we actually saw some trees beginning to bud. On the very last day of May, in the afternoon, I reached Brunswick House. It is situated on a beautiful lake, the whole establishment consisting of about five or six houses; it is a fur-trading post. The Indians speak the Saulteaux language; there are about a hundred and fifty of them here; they are quiet and teachable, but given to pilfering and very superstitious. To comfort they seem to be strangers, lying about anywhere at night, their principal resort being the platforms near the trading-house. I believe that God's blessing rested on my labours among these Indians. This was their first introduction to the Christian religion, and I trust that ere long many will be numbered among Christ's disciples.

'After remaining with them nine days, I was obliged to hurry northward. Our progress was rapid, the water was in good order. A few days at Moose, and I went to the sea-coast to Rupert's House. I found between three and four hundred Indians assembled there, under the guidance of their teacher, Matamashkum. Our joy was great and mutual; they have been heathens, many of them have committed horrible crimes, but those days have passed away, and now they rejoice in the merits of a Crucified Saviour. Twice every day we had service, almost out of doors, for there was no available room at the place capable of containing all. During the day I had examinations, and baptisms, and weddings, and consultations; and one afternoon we had a grand feast, for the Indians had made a good hunt, and the fur-traders, delighted with what they had done, provided the feast for them. There was nothing of dissipation. Eating and drinking was quite a serious matter with them, and it was astonishing to see the quantities of pea-soup, pork, geese, bread, biscuit, tobacco, tea and sugar, they consumed; the providing a body of Indians with a good feast is no light matter.

'Having spent two Sundays at Rupert's House, I took canoe and went to Fort George, northwards along the sea-coast. For a portion of the way I had company, as many Indians were also going north.

This was the most pleasant of all the journeys; the weather fine, the scenery often grand, the wind fair. Two hundred miles were made in four days and a half. At Fort George I met a good body of Christian Indians with their teacher, William Keshkumash.

'A few days here, and I embarked on board a schooner, to go yet further north, to Great Whale River. Soon after getting out to sea we were among the ice; however, on we go. It is the sea, but there is no water! We are in an Arctic scene; we cannot go through, so we turn our head for Fort George again, and wait there for nearly another week, and then try once more. We get half way, then, as the vessel cannot move forward, I leave it, and accompanied by two native sailors proceed in a small boat. Two days bring us to an encampment of Indians. I now leave my boat and enter a canoe, having with me Keshkumash, his wife, and their young son; two other canoes, each containing a man and his wife, keep us company. We have to work in earnest. Sometimes we got along fast, then we were in the midst of ice and could not move at all, again we were chopping a passage for the canoe with our axes; and then, when we could do nothing else, we carried it over the rocks and set it down where the ice was not so closely packed.

'After two days and a half of this we came to a standstill, and I determined to go on foot. I took one Indian with me, and we set off. Our walk was over high bare hills; rivers ran through several of the valleys, these we waded. About ten o'clock that night I sat down once more in a house, very, very tired, and very, very thankful. I spent several days with the Indians of this place ; they are a large tribe of Crees, but speak somewhat differently from those of Moose. Most of them believed the words that were spoken, but some cared for none of those things, being filled with their own superstitions.

'By-and-by the schooner Fox made her appearance, and I embarked once more, to endeavour to get to the last inhabited spot, Little Whale River. We went half way, and then the ice sent a hole through the Fox's side; this we covered with a sheet of lead. I now again deserted the Fox, and took to the canoe, in which, in somewhat less than two days, I got at last to my journey's end. And that journey's end is a dreary, dreary place, with scarcely any summer. It was August, and the ice was lying thick at the mouth of the river. But my work was not dreary. I here met Eskimo, the most teachable of people. They were very ready for school or service, and although their attainments were not high, so much was I impressed with their sincerity and perseverance, that I admitted four families into the Christian Church. This rewarded me for all my toil. I can address them now as brothers and sisters ; and I am sure that all my friends will rejoice with me for the blessing with which God crowned my labour.

'I had my difficulties in getting back again; ice still disputed our progress, but on August 30, late in the evening, the trusty Fox, battered and bruised, came to anchor at Moose Factory, and I had the happiness of once more meeting my family, and of finding that all had been quite well during the whole of my absence.'

About this time Mr. Horden began to plead for help to train up one of the most promising of his school-boys as a catechist. Friends of the Coral Fund took up the lad, and the money expended upon his education was not in vain, for that boy is now a native pastor in charge of Rupert's House. Of him and of his ordination we shall have more to relate by-and-by. The school children in whom Mr. Horden had first taken an interest were growing up. Some were already earning their living, some were married; one girl had gone with her husband to the Red River settlement, and was, wrote Mr. Horden, in 1869, in as respectable a sphere of life as any Christian farmer's wife in England could be. Another had married a fine young Moose Fort hunter, an excellent voyager. After an absence of several months, they with their little child came back to the place, stayed a few days, and again departed. In May, at the breaking-up of the river, the Indians came in. One canoe Mr. Horden felt sure was that of Amelia and her husband, and he at once went to see them.

'I saw,' he says, 'first a fair little boy, plump and hearty, showing that great care had been taken of him. I then cast my eye on a woman sitting near, whom I took to be a stranger; but another look showed me that the poor emaciated creature was indeed none other than Amelia, who had been brought to the brink of the grave by starvation. She had lost her husband, but in all her privations she had taken care that her baby son should not want. The tale of her suffering was very distressing. After leaving Moose in the end of March, they by themselves had gone to their hunting-grounds, hoping to get a few furs to pay off the debt they had contracted with the fur-trader; for in the early part of the winter they had been very unfortunate, a wolverine having destroyed nearly all the martens they had trapped. Amelia's husband was soon attacked by sickness, which entirely laid him by; food was very scarce, and the little the forest might yield he could not seek. He gradually became worse and worse, his sufferings aggravated by want, his only source of consolation was his religion; both expected to lay their bones, as well as those of the child, where they were. He wrote a letter, and got Amelia to go and hang it up where some Indians might pass in the summer, stating their joint deaths and the cause, and requesting burial. The end came, the once strong young man lay a corpse; but Amelia had something to live for—for her little son she would struggle on. Unable to dig a grave, for she had no strength and the ground was frozen as hard as a stone, she covered the body with moss, and set off to the Main Moose River, hoping there to fall in with Indians. She was not disappointed. After a while she fell in with Isaac Mekawatch, a Moose Indian, who took care of her and her child, and brought them in safety to the fort. Such incidents as this are amongst the sad experiences of life in Moosonee.'

In 1870 Mr. Horden wrote: 'I have this summer travelled about thirteen hundred miles, and during a part of this time I experienced a considerable degree of hardship, which brought me down greatly. I am now, however, well as ever I have been in my life. It was a very long journey, and occupied many weeks, yet I did not travel out of my parish all the time. When I was at Matawakumma, five hundred miles south of Moose, I was upwards of eleven hundred miles from Little Whale River.

'I left Moose on June 13, and overtook a boat going to the Long Portage, with goods for the supply of New Brunswick, and I went forward in it. Travelling by boat is very monotonous work indeed. At breakfast-time, dinner-time, and when the day's work was done, we endeavoured to catch a few fish, our rod a long rough stick cut from the woods, a piece of strong cord for a line, to which we attached a large hook baited with salt pork; with this we would occasionally draw out a perch, a trout, a pike from six to twelve pounds in weight. At the Long Portage I changed my mode of travelling, my companions now using the canoe. With my new friends I got on extremely well, taking advantage of every opportunity to instruct them in divine things. Most of them received the instruction gladly, but a few held back; they love their old superstitions, their conjurations, dreams, spirits, and all the other things which so sadly debase the Indian mind. In due time New Brunswick was reached, and I at once began my work.

'The Indians here, before they had ever seen a missionary, used to meet for prayer and exhortation, having learnt a little from an Indian who had seen one. Desirous of knowing how they conducted their service, about which I had heard a great deal, I arranged one evening to be present as a spectator. They showed no shyness, but consented at once.

'At the time appointed, all being assembled, one gave out the verse of a hymn, which was sung by all; another then repeated a text of Scripture, then a second verse of the hymn was sung, followed by a second text; all then knelt down, I by the side of the old chief, and about six began to pray aloud at the same time, each in his own words. Ojibway's prayer was very simple, of course, but it was a cry to Jesus for mercy; and can we doubt that his prayer was heard? Kneeling by his side was one sent by God to show him the way of salvation.

'One of those who opposed the Gospel said: "I would not give up my children to you for baptism on any account. My eldest child has been twice so ill that I thought she would die, but an Indian, by his charms, saved her; and recently a spirit appeared to me, telling me to take heed and never give up my children, for if I did, he would no longer take care of them, and they would die."

'I remained at Brunswick until the Indians departed to Michipicoton for supplies of flour. I went with them a little way, and then on to Flying Post by a road untrodden by any save the Indian on his hunting expeditions. I found it a terrible route—the worst I have ever travelled—but having no one to think of but myself, I did not mind it—I was about my Master's business. In due time we reached Flying Post. Our last portage was eight miles of truly horrible walking; it cost us many weary hours.

'The Indians of Flying Post evinced a great desire for instruction. This was my first visit; I baptized seventeen persons. From Flying Post I went on to Matawakumma. At Matawakumma the Indians are decreasing, as at Flying Post. The decay of a people brings sad reflections, and the Indians seem doomed to extinction. I found a church partly built under the guidance of their trader, Mr. Richards, who takes a deep interest in his Indians' welfare. A bell and a set of communion plate I hope to get out next ship time; the little church in the wilderness will then be tolerably well furnished.

'I here made the largest comparative collection I have ever made in my life, no less than 8*l.* 2*s.* 8*d.* The poor people were truly liberal in their poverty, and some of these poor sheep for the first time approached the table of the Lord. Some of them are very intelligent, can read well, and thoroughly understand their Christian responsibilities and appreciate their privileges. And now, my work done, I turn my canoe-head Mooseward, and pass over grand lakes, down a large river, run the rapids, admire the falls, carry over the portages, hurrying towards the sea, and after an absence of between eight and nine weeks I found myself once more in the bosom of my family.'

CHAPTER IX

DAYS OF LABOUR

NOTHING perhaps could give a better idea of Mr. Horden's gigantic labours than an account of a day's work at different times. A Sunday in the winter of 1871 is thus spent by him.

'While it was yet dark,' he says, 'at half-past six o'clock the church bells summoned us to the house of prayer; the cold was severe, but I found a tolerable congregation awaiting me, and the service was very enjoyable. The congregation dismissed, I returned home to breakfast, and soon afterwards went to the church again for our English service. This is conducted precisely as in a church at home; the full service is read, and we use one prayer which you do not, for the Governor-General of Canada and the Lieutenant-Governor of the Hudson's Bay Territories. The congregation is composed of the deputy-governor, his family and his staff of clerks, and the doctor—not one of whom is ever absent, and all but one are communicants—my own family, and the servants European and native of the Hudson's Bay Company. After the sermon a general offertory was made, and then the communicants met around the

Lord's table, there to renew their vows, and to partake of that spiritual food which was ordained to strengthen them in their heavenly course.

'At a quarter to two the bell was rung for school, and a few minutes after I was with the scholars, on my knees seeking a blessing on our meeting together. School over, our second Indian service commenced with a larger congregation than in the early morning, for young children can be brought out now. There is again a departure from the church, yet some remain, and those, as their English-speaking brethren had done in the morning, commemorate their dying Saviour's love. In all thirty have communicated. The shades of evening are falling as I leave the church, after a fatiguing, but blessed day's work.'

The necessity was laid upon Mr. Horden of being like St. Paul, 'in journeyings oft,' and the day's work we have now to speak of was one of journeying.

'Last summer,' he says, 'I was on my way to Rupert's House. A large boat just built was going there, and I took a passage in it. It was loaded with a miscellaneous cargo of bricks, potatoes, a stove, bags of flour, and bales of goods. The crew was composed of Rupert's House Indians, fine manly fellows, and all Christians. Leaving Moose somewhat late in the day, we went but a short distance and encamped on an island, eight miles off, called Ship-sands. Here we set up our tent and cooked our supper; then we gathered together, and joined our voices in a hymn of praise. I read a portion of Scripture, and we all knelt in prayer to the God of heaven and earth, and not long after lay down to rest. At midnight there was an arrival, and I was aroused from sleep by my guide, with the cry of "Musenahekun! Musenahekun!" A packet! a packet! These are magic words. I started to my feet in an instant, for not since February had I seen a letter from home, and it was now June 17. It was, however, but a poor affair, containing no private letters from England, and but little public news. The real packet I welcomed at Rupert's House nearly a month later.

'In the early morn we spread our sails to the wind and went joyously forward. The east point of Hannah Bay is reached, and it now seems that further progress is impossible; there is ice, ice; block after block is pushed aside; hoisting sail, back we go, to round a projecting point. We are in a narrow, crooked lane of water, through which we move very carefully, with poles in hand, ready to do battle with any piece of ice which lies in our way, and so hour after hour slips by, and all hopes of reaching Rupert's House are at an end; but towards evening our labours are crowned with success, and the clear sea stretches before us. There is no place to land. We set our best man at the helm, and taking reefs in our sails, trust to the protection of the Almighty. I think it was the most uncomfortable night I have ever spent.

'In the early morning the wind abated. We once more set sail, and traversed beautiful Rupert's Bay, with its varied scenery of hill and valley, wooded headlands and bare rocks, Gheiles Mount, the highest eminence in this part of the country, rising majestically above all. By and by, the North Point is reached, and we enter Rupert's River. We have been seen at Rupert's House, the flag is waving in the breeze; the few houses form a pretty picture in the morning light; and just before seven o'clock I am heartily welcomed by a crowd of Europeans and natives, who come down to the river's bank to meet me, as I get out of the boat.'

Rupert's House is an important post of the Hudson's Bay Company, and the centre of their fur trade in a very extensive district. The business is managed by a trader high in the Hudson's Bay service, assisted by a clerk, a storekeeper, and a staff of tradesmen and servants; the buildings consist of the master's residence, houses for the servants, large and substantially built stores, and last, though not least, a capacious church. 'That church,' says Mr. Horden, 'how long I had sighed for it; how hard I had laboured one summer getting logs brought to the place from distant woods, and sawn into boards for the commencement of the building! And now I see a stream of worshippers flowing from tents and marquees, gradually filling it, until there is scarcely room for another human being. What joy and gratitude did I feel! This is the fifth church in my district since Moose became my home; my next must be four hundred miles from Rupert's House, for the Saulteaux Indians of New Brunswick.

'There goes the bell! it is just six o'clock. I had service every morning at Rupert's House, but this morning there is an innovation, I am one of the assembly, not the leader; I have deputed an Indian to conduct the service, and right well he performs his duty. The Litany is very impressively rendered, and a chapter of St. Matthew well read. The numerous voices mingle in their translation of "He dies, the friend of sinners dies"—*Nepeu, umra ka sakehat*—to Luther's hymn; then I take the Testament and once more read the chapter and explain it, enforcing its lessons on my hearers; the hymn, "Lord, dismiss us with Thy blessing," is sung, and the congregation separates.

'It is time for breakfast. I take mine with my kind host, the trader, who is not only an English gentleman, but a Churchman and communicant. At nine o'clock I am in my vestry, and around me are the servants' children. I am in a small English school, reading the English Testament, teaching English hymns, till eleven, when my Indians come to me family by family.

'Here is Jacob Matamashkum.

'"Well, Jacob, how did you get on last winter?"

'"Part of it very badly, part tolerably well. It was a poor season for furs, martens entirely failed, and none of the other animals made up for the deficiency; many of the Indians will be quite unable to pay their debts to the trader. We had our prayers every day, and we kept the Sabbath, but once now and then we were obliged to look for some food on Sunday when we had nothing. We love our religion more and more, and are very glad indeed we have the church to assemble in."

'Then I gave my instructions, assured that, as far as possible, they would be attended to. And so the hours passed by. At four o'clock I had a very solemn service; two gentlemen, one more than seventy years of age, and the other in middle life, both from far in the interior of the country, knelt together for the first time in their lives at the Lord's table; the elder had not seen a clergyman for upwards of a quarter of a century. At six o'clock it is ding-dong, ding-dong, again, and again the voice of praise is raised, prayer offered, the Bible read and explained, and the congregation then separated to their fragile and temporary dwellings. Yet once more the bell calls to prayer; the master, the gentlemen from the interior, the servants, their wives and children obey the summons, and I hold an English service, enjoyable and enjoyed. At its termination I take a short walk, reflecting on the day's events, offering up a silent prayer that God would vouchsafe His blessing thereon abundantly.'

CHAPTER X

THE BISHOPRIC OF MOOSONEE

THE summer of 1872 passed. On September 13 of that year Mr. Horden wrote to the present writer: 'Your much prized letter reached me a day or two before I set out on one of my longest and most trying journeys, from which I have but just returned. I took your letter with me, and indulged myself with an occasional perusal of it; it has been to many of the posts of the country, has journeyed over some of our terrible portages, and has sailed over many a lake through the "forgotten land," as it may well be called, for it is waiting, and will long wait, to be taken possession of. The Indians cannot be said to hold possession, they are so few in number, and the country is so vast, that one unacquainted with it can have no conception of its extent. Fancy travelling a whole fortnight, and during that time not seeing one hundred persons. A feeling of great sadness sometimes crept over me as my solitary canoe glided over the bosom of some beautiful sea-like lake; myself and canoe-men were alone in the wilderness. I shall (D.V.) write you again in February, when I hope to send you as usual a "little budget."'

Little did the hero of our history imagine when he wrote those last lines that a new era was even then about to open in his eventful life. Our readers, who have thus far followed his steps with interest, will learn, we feel assured, with heartfelt sympathy, that the well-tried and devoted missionary, the faithful friend and pastor of his flock during so many years, was now to become the missionary bishop of the newly-formed diocese of Moosonee, formerly a portion of the enormous diocese of Rupertsland. At short notice he started for England, leaving wife and children at Moose, for he was not to be long absent. He was consecrated at Westminster Abbey on December 15, 1872.

In the few short months which he spent at home the new bishop pleaded hard, and not without response, for assistance to carry out his plans for advancing and consolidating his former work in what was henceforth to be his diocese, stretching 1,500 miles from east to west and north to south, inhabited by Crees, Ojibbeways and Eskimo, together with some Europeans and half-castes. As a missionary he had the joy of witnessing the conversion of the greater part of those children of the wilderness, and now, as a missionary bishop, his heart was set on the raising up of a native ministry, supported as far as possible by native resources.

In this some progress had already been made. His plan was to divide the diocese into five districts, each of them superintended by a fully qualified pastor, who would be assisted by two or three other

Indian clergymen, whose training would be confined to a thorough knowledge of their Bibles and Prayer-books in their own language. These men would accompany the members of their own tribes to their hunting-grounds, and as they would be able in a great measure to support themselves, they would require but a comparatively small allowance for their maintenance. This was his purpose, and what he purposed he had with the Divine assistance, which he ever sought, never yet failed to carry out.

All praise to Thee, my Father and my God.
Thus far Thy love has brought me on life's road;
Day after day Thy mercy was renewed,
Night after night my safety been secured.

. . . . . .

More like to Jesus I would daily grow,
Through whom redemption, love, and mercy flow;
More loving, holy, generous, resigned,
Thoughtless of self, the friend of all mankind.

Thus was the newly consecrated bishop moved to sing.

At home in Moose again, with his dear wife and children, Bishop Horden hastened to buckle to his beloved work; but he found time to write a graphic account of his homeward journey, in which he had as his companion his second daughter, who had just left school; the eldest was already at Moose. They travelled *viâ* New York to Michipicoton, and thence the remainder of the long, long journey by canoe, 'encamping,' wrote the bishop, 'in woods under a canvas marquee, waited on by Indians, travelling through perfect solitudes for days without seeing any human being other than our crew. It was on the morning of Tuesday, July 8, that we stepped into our canoe, having four Indian companions. We went up the river slowly against the stream. Then came a long portage, where we carried everything, and this detained us many hours; then on and on till night. Then we put ashore, lit our fire, erected our tent, fried our pancakes, boiled our kettles, made our beds, and having partaken of a good supper, we assembled our men around us, and they knelt in prayer to the Father in heaven; then, shutting the tent's frail door, we lay down to rest.

'The feeling was strange: so many months had elapsed since the ground had been my bed. Sleep did not come at once, and thoughts were busy on the past and the future. Presently I slept soundly until the early morn, when we were awakened to pursue our way. We were off by five o'clock, and during the day travelled mostly among large lakes. There were no birds, no creatures of any kind visible, except when we were crossing the portages, and here we saw quite enough of the dreaded mosquito. On the third day we came upon two men engaged in erecting a house, which was to be a trading post in opposition to the great traders of the country, the Hudson's Bay Company. On our fifth night, when we were not very far from New Brunswick, we were so troubled by mosquitoes that we could get no sleep, and we were not at all sorry when the light of the early morn allowed us to pursue our way over a bare and swampy portage.

'This ended, we once more got into our canoe, and in a few hours found ourselves at the little post of New Brunswick. Here were some Indians, but not very many, and with them I spent the day, praying with and teaching them. They are as yet mere infants in the faith, knowing but little; but I would fain hope that much good has been already effected by the preaching of the Gospel. They were very low, but some among them have already been baptized, and are walking consistently. The new trader they have among them is an old friend, who takes deep interest in the spiritual welfare of those who come to him for the purposes of trade.

'Work done, we once more entered our canoe, passed through Brunswick Lake out into the broad Brunswick branch of the Moose River, and here our real troubles began. It rained heavily for several days. It was bad enough in the canoe, but it was much worse on the portages. Fancy a narrow rough path through the woods, with thick bushes on either side, and the path deep in mud and water. I was much afraid my dear daughter Chrissie would suffer from such exposure, but she bore up cheerfully, and proved herself an expert traveller.

'When the portages were passed we had 150 miles further to go; but the wind became fair, and we almost flew over the water. On Tuesday morning, July 22, we rounded the head of Moose Island, and our home stood before us. There was a great running and calling, and a hoisting of flags. The guns gave their loud welcome, and the dear ones who had been left behind came out to greet us; and there was joy—deep, oh, how deep and grateful! for God had indeed dealt very graciously with us. Our first evening passed. It has left the impression of a pleasant dream. I cannot record our sayings and doings—our exclamations, our tones of joy and sorrow as we spoke of this friend's success, or that one's distress: of this one being born, and that one dying; it was an evening unique in our history. We had no "pemmican," for we are not in the land of the buffalo; it is an article of food unknown here. Neither had we "salt goose," a viand which takes the place of the pemmican; we had something better for that evening!

'I at once set to work; life is too short and precious to waste much of it; and since then every day has been crowded. I sometimes scarcely know what to do first, and yet I find time to sit down and write a line or two to a friend. The way I manage it is this. I get my work of translation forward by devoting to it a few extra hours daily, knowing that a packet time will come, and that it is necessary that every hour of packet week must be given up to writing; the bonds of Christian friendship must not be lightly broken. The translation work is very heavy and trying. This is what I have accomplished since I returned in July: I have revised our Indian hymn-book, adding to it a large number of new hymns. I have translated all the first lessons between the tenth Sunday after Trinity and the first Sunday in Lent, as well as some for many of the holy days. What I wish to accomplish is the

Psalter, the first lessons, and the New Testament, to be bound up in one volume. If I go on as I have done, I may get the whole ready in twelve months from this time. I shall give myself no rest until my people have the whole of the Word of God in their hands.'

Thus the good bishop worked on, happy in the conviction that if things were not hurrying onward to perfection, they were at least moving slowly in the right direction—his exertions being helped by his Heavenly Father, to whom he attributed all progress.

CHAPTER XI

A PICNIC AND AN INDIAN DANCE

THE year 1874 was an eventful one at Moose; the breaking-up of the ice brought with it a flood, and the bishop and his family had to be fetched in a canoe to the house of the deputy-governor for safety. The moving ice masses tore up the river bank, broke down the fences, snapped trees as if they had been reeds; whilst an incessant roar was kept up as the mile-wide river rushed madly on towards the sea. Crops were backward and sparse that season.

In July the bishop started on his summer visitation tour to Rupert's House, East Main, and Fort George. Everywhere he was received with open arms; everywhere the services were well attended; at each of the posts visited many were baptized and confirmed.

By September the bishop was back again, busy amongst his Indians and with the European sailors who had spent perforce a whole year in the vicinity, the ship of 1873 having been ice-bound off Charlton Island; there was no place nearer at hand at which she could winter in safety. But the captain, mate, and some of the men had visited Moose during the summer, and every opportunity of communication had been taken advantage of. Now they were occupied in cleaning the ship and making ready for a fresh start homewards. Late one night, just before she set sail, the bishop and his wife accompanied their newly-married daughter on board, their eldest —the child whom Bishop Anderson had baptized. All hands were invited aft; a last solemn and affecting farewell service was held.

The annual ship came and went, and the good folks at Moose began to feel at once that winter was at the door. The weather, though still warm, could not be long depended upon. 'We begin,' wrote the bishop, 'to take up our potatoes; that done, we look well to our buildings, to prevent as far as possible the entrance of frost; then we endeavour to lay in a stock of fish for the winter, some of which are salted while others are frozen—in which state they keep good almost all the winter; after that, pigs and cattle are killed, and cut up, and allowed to freeze. Then the great labour of the season begins—the cutting and hauling of firewood, for we have no coals here. We send men armed with large axes into the thick woods, and there they chop down tree after tree, strip off the branches, cut them into billets about three feet long, split them and pile them into a "cord." A cord is a pile of billets eight feet long and four feet high, one and a half of such being considered a fair day's work for a man. Then other men come with horses and oxen, harnessed to sledges, and haul the wood to our respective houses, near which it is repiled. Then the men are sent further off to get logs for building purposes, which are rafted down the river on the breaking-up of the ice.

'My young son Bertie delights in chopping, and in winter both Bertie and Beatrice delight in tobogganing, which gives them capital exercise. A piece of wood about six feet long, ten inches broad, and a quarter of an inch thick, is turned up a little in front, and is then called a sled; this is brought to the edge of the river's bank, which is in some places very steep. Bertie sits down in front, armed with a short stick to guide the sled; his sister sits down behind him, and down they rush with amazing speed, the impetus carrying them far out on the frozen river; then they trudge up the bank, bringing the sled with them, and the process is repeated again and again. As this sort of exercise is a little too violent for a person of middle age, I don't engage in it now. Then there is the fishing. Walking out two or three miles in snow-shoes, a gipsy tent is made in the woods; holes are cut in the thick ice, a pile of pine brush is brought from the woods; and then comes the sitting and shivering at the hole, bobbing a baited hook up and down, perhaps the pleasure of catching a fish, then the pleasure of cooking it, and then the pleasure of eating it.'

During the cold of this year's winter the bishop allowed himself a rare holiday—the only one, indeed, with the exception of those connected with Christmas-tree doings, ever recorded by him in his many letters to us. Availing himself of an unusually fine warm day in February, he held a grand picnic with his family and friends, driving out four or five miles in dog and horse sleighs, taking dinner in a large comfortable tent, with a fine fire in the centre, and then going down to the river and fishing through holes cut in the ice. 'Bobbing our hooks, baited with either a piece of fat pork or rabbit, until a hungry trout made a dart at it, we generally succeeded,' he says, 'in drawing it through the thick ice on to the snow, where in a short time he became frozen hard; for when I say that we had a warm day, I mean the thermometer stood but a little below zero.' Yes, there sat the bishop and his children and friends on pine brush on the ice, quite enjoying themselves!

'We got home very nicely in the evening, but the cold was then becoming severe, and as the wind was high we should have been very uncomfortable indeed had we been out much later. With all the drawbacks, I am very happy here at Moose. I have no time for *kushkaletumowin*, or "thinking long." Were the day thirty hours instead of twenty-four, I should still find it too short. Each year finds me busier than its predecessor, and so I suppose it will continue to the end. The happiest man is he who is most diligently employed about his Master's business. I have before me for next summer a most extensive journey; I go to Red River to attend the first meeting of our provincial synod, and then to York Factory, travelling over four thousand miles.'

The school, under the bishop's own immediate superintendence, was going on well, the scholars making good progress. One boy, out of school hours, was employed in chopping wood for the school fire. Another had accompanied the bishop in all his last summer journeyings, behaving in an exemplary manner. A third, Edward Richards, was already very useful, assisting as a master in the school. The Indians are very fond of their children, and perhaps a little over-indulgent. The spoilt children are sometimes disobedient. The bishop gives an amusing description of parental admonition on one occasion at a distant camp. 'I had been,' he says, 'away from home for some time, and hoped before night to arrive at East Main. I had reached a part of the coast opposite the large island Wepechenite, "the Walrus," when I observed a body of Indians standing on a rock, watching us. Here was an opportunity not to be missed; those Indians might not hear the Gospel again for years. I at once directed my men to look out for a good landing-place, and I got ashore. My men also came ashore, and began collecting wood for the purpose of cooking breakfast. In the meantime the Indians, seeing our movements, got their canoes into the water; they did not come empty-handed, but brought a large number of fine white fish, called by them Atikamakwuk—"deer of the sea," some dried, others fresh, just taken from the nets. I collected all our visitors to a service, at which many children were to be baptized. The deepest attention was paid. The morning hymn was heartily sung, for these Indians are all Christians. The discourse is being delivered when there is a great stir among the congregation ; faces look excited, voices are raised, apparently in anger. For a moment I was at a loss to account for this ; then I saw that it was my address that was taking effect, although not quite in the way I had intended. I was speaking to the young people, telling them their duty to their parents. The mothers thought this an opportunity not to be passed over, so, raising their voices, they cried out to their daughters, "Do you hear? Isn't this what we are always telling you?" Then, rushing at them, they brought them to the front, saying, "Come here, that he may see you ; let him see how ashamed you look, you disobedient children!" Turning to me they said, "Yes, they are disobedient, they will not listen ; perhaps now they have heard you they will behave better." The young people promised better conduct for the future. The service over, we once more took to our canoe, and paddled on under the hottest sun, I think, I have ever experienced.'

It was during this summer trip that the bishop witnessed an Indian dance.

'I had travelled far,' he says. 'I had visited the stations on the East Main coast, and had been some time at Little Whale River. It is a dreary place, and the mighty, frowning, rocky portals of the river seem fitted for the entrance to other regions, to another world. I had spent much time preaching the Gospel to Europeans, half-castes, Indians, and Eskimo, and I was intending almost immediately to turn the bow of my canoe southwards, and speed back as fast as possible to my home at Moose Factory.

'Walking out one evening with the gentleman in charge of the post, we were somewhat startled by a great noise proceeding from an encampment of Indians a quarter of a mile distant, on the top of a high hill. "A conjuring, a conjuring extraordinary!" said we. We ascended the hill quietly, and quite unobserved. Having attained the summit, we walked rapidly towards a large tent from which the noise was proceeding, and looked in, but at first could make out nothing distinctly. We entered, and found six or seven men standing as closely together as possible around a very small fire, dancing, or rather shuffling up and down, without in the least changing their position; the women and children were sitting around, admiring and applauding spectators of the doings of their lords and masters. There was music, too, both vocal and instrumental. The player was likewise the vocalist; he was an old man, who sat among the women and children; his instrument an old kettle, over which a piece of deer-skin had been tightly drawn, and this he beat with a stick, accompanying with his cracked voice, raised to its highest pitch. The dancing and music continued for some hours, but about every five minutes there was a momentary cessation, when all in the tent joined in a prolonged howl. All seemed to thoroughly enjoy the sport, and I was myself glad to see it, for it was no conjuring after all, only a little simple amusement, and it was the first sign of animation I had witnessed among those Indians, who are not of a very high type of humanity. They are now all Christians, but the standard of Christianity is low—

how can it be otherwise? I am the nearest clergyman to them, and I am six hundred miles distant. The difficulty of reaching them is very great, for the sea in their vicinity is open but for a short time in the whole year. This summer I had hoped to see a labourer stationed among them and the teachable Eskimo, but for the present I have been disappointed.'

The bishop's thoughts were much occupied with the need for more churches and schools, more pastors and teachers, in his extensive diocese. In 1875 he writes: 'At present there are three clergymen in the diocese besides myself, and the work we have to do is very great and onerous. I have given, God's grace enabling me to do so, more than twenty years of my life to the cause which is so close to my heart, and I long to see the whole of the country under my charge not only free from superstition, but likewise entirely under the sway of Christ, that there shall not be a tribe, either among the Crees, Ojibbeways, or Eskimo, which has not its well-instructed and fully-accredited teacher. Many of the tribes do not see a minister's face for years.'

Bishop Horden had now been actively engaged in the mission field nearly a quarter of a century. On January 6, 1876, he writes: 'During the whole of that time I have not been laid up with any serious illness whatever, and I am thankful to add that I still feel as strong in body and as capable of work as when I first landed here; truly God has surrounded me with loving-kindness and tender mercy; but in the course of last year He taught me, in a manner not to be misunderstood, that the threads of my life are held in His hand, for He plucked me from the very jaws of death.

'With a large number of fellow-passengers I was on board the steamship Manitoba, on Lake Superior, on my way to Michipicoton, when late in the evening we came into collision with the American steamship the Comet, a vessel more than twice the size of our own, laden with a heavy cargo of silver ore and pig-iron. That we escaped without material injury seemed quite miraculous, for the Comet sank immediately, and with her, I am grieved to add, eleven of her crew of twenty-one men. I trust that this nearness to death, showing me how uncertain is life, is causing me to value it more highly, and to labour more earnestly in the vineyard before the night cometh in which no man can work.'

CHAPTER XII

ORGANISATION AND TRAVEL

THE marked feature of the year 1875 was the organisation of the four dioceses, into which the old diocese of Rupertsland was divided, into an ecclesiastical province, the first synod of which was held in the beginning of August. This necessitated the bishop's going to Winnipeg, Red River, a journey of fifteen hundred miles. 'In going I visited the stations of New Brunswick, Misenabe, and Michipicoton. At New Brunswick much progress is being made; most of the Indians are now baptized, and as the present agent of the Hudson's Bay Company there is a great friend of missions, and one who will do all in his power for the spiritual benefit of those attached to his trading post, I hope it will not be long before heathenism will have taken its entire departure, and Christianity be the professed religion of that important portion of my charge. From all the stations I receive good reports, but before that advance can be made for which we so deeply long, we must have more labourers. We are so few, and the field is so large. In the autumn the mission was strengthened by the arrival of the Rev. J. H. Keen from England, and a valuable gift he is proving himself to be. I trust another man equally good will be sent next autumn.

'In May I hope to set apart Mr. Saunders, a native of the country, for the work of the ministry among his countrymen (the Ojibbeways). Thus I shall be enabled to occupy three most important posts, so that, should I further carry out my plans, I shall consider that I have the diocese tolerably well in hand. The places I hope to occupy are Rupert's House, to which an immense extent of country looks as its head; Matawakumma, which will guard the frontier from Roman Catholic encroachment; and Whale River, opening up communication with the interesting but much neglected Eskimo of the north-eastern coast of Hudson's Bay. Another place, Flying Post, I had likewise hoped to supply with a permanent competent teacher, but the man intended for it, a pure Indian, will not be ready this year.'

The Rev. J. H. Keen had been assisting the bishop at Moose, but the people at Rupert's House were still without a missionary, so at Christmas he was given up to them, and the bishop took the work at Moose Fort alone. The Christmas Day services began ere the stars had disappeared from the firmament, and continued till late in the afternoon. 'After this,' he writes, 'I felt considerably fatigued, but a cup of tea revived me, and I spent a quietly happy evening with my wife and youngest children.'

In the following summer the bishop joined Mr. Keen at Rupert's House. 'Among those who came down to meet me,' he says, 'were our old friends Matamashkum, Wapunaweshkum, Snuffers, and many others. Our joy was mutual.

'Soon arrived the brigades from Mistasinnce, Waswanepe, and Nitchekwun, hundreds of miles up the Rupert's River. We were busy morning, noon, and night. Every moment was employed, for these children of ours would have but a few days' intercourse with their father, and then would again return to their distant homes. We had marriages to perform, many children to baptize, candidates for confirmation to prepare, communicants to instruct, the disobedient to rebuke. There was not much of this, however, and the days ran rapidly and happily on. The Psalter, beautifully printed from my translation, had come to us the previous ship time, and the Indians were delighted. After a little while it was most cheering to hear how well they read together their appointed portions. They gave me a very good collection, a good number of beaver; that is to say, they did not give me a large pile of beaver skins, but our native teacher, Jacob Matamashkum, had made a list of all the Indians, and after each name he had written down the man's contribution in beaver. When the list was completed it was given to the resident trader, who credited me with three shillings for each beaver. Altogether it amounted to a considerable sum.'

Some time after this the bishop made a voyage in the Mink to Big River and Great Whale River, both on the eastern coast of Hudson's Bay. At Great Whale River the work was of a varied character, amongst Indians, Eskimo, and English. The Eskimo were assembled in some numbers for the whale fishery. But it was not a success that season. The whales, or rather porpoises, remained outside the river, and would not come in. 'A whale fishery when the whales are numerous is a very exciting sight. I myself,' says the bishop, 'have engaged in a fishery in which a thousand were killed, but that was many years ago. The Eskimo gave much cause for encouragement; no matter what they were about, when summoned to school or service the work was dropped instantly, their little books were taken up, and off they trotted, singing, listening, praying; they showed that they were thoroughly in earnest.'

'How grieved was my heart that I had no one to leave behind who might take the Eskimo as his special charge!' says the bishop. But the man desired was even then approaching Moose Fort in the annual ship. It was Mr. Peck, a layman, who had spent some of the earlier years of his life as a sailor. 'It was by searching the Scriptures in my mess on board one of H.M.'s vessels that the light shone into my darkened soul; it was then I knew its truth,' he says. The bishop was much pleased with the earnestness and evident fitness for the work of the young missionary. After remaining at Moose only a week, the latter set out in a boat with three or four Indians for his distant and lonely home. After a few months he returned to Moose to be ordained.

'The two events of the winter,' writes the bishop, February 1878, 'have been the children's school-treat and the ordination of Mr. Peck. The treat was a great success. Fifty-six partook of our hospitality. We divided them into two parties on two successive evenings; I never saw children enjoy themselves more. We had many games to amuse them, finishing each evening with a religious service. Edward Richards, one of the Coral Fund *protégés*, is with us, assisting generally in the mission. He has done good work this winter in giving instruction to Mr. Peck in the Indian language. My son is spending the winter with us, cheering us much, and assisting in the work. In the summer he takes his mother, Beatrice, and Bertie to England, the two latter to go to school. I am afraid I shall find a bachelor's life here rather hard.'

On May 10, 1878, the bishop, with heartfelt thanksgiving, ordained Mr. Peck deacon and priest. 'He left us,' writes Mr. Horden on June 18, 'with our deepest sympathy and our most earnest prayers. He left us well prepared for his work, and with a good insight into the two difficult native languages he will be in constant contact with, the Cree and the Eskimo. He is full of zeal—zeal tempered with prudence, and I think that, should his life be spared, a noble career is before him. The surroundings of his home are very desolate, and he needs all the help and sympathy we can give him.'

This summer was spent as usual in almost constant travel by the bishop, who still had not been from end to end of his vast diocese. The station next in importance to Moose at that time was York Factory, but he had never yet seen it, owing to the great distance. This summer he visited Albany. Although it was the end of June, ice was still lying on the coast when he set out in a large canoe, accompanied by six Indians. The way lay along the western shore of James' Bay. The scenery is very dreary, the coast low and flat, not a hill to be seen. At the end of three days he found himself 'at a very small village, consisting of the residence of the fur trader, a nice church, a good parsonage, a few well-built houses, and a number of Indian tents.'

'I was most heartily welcomed,' he writes. 'It was late in the evening when I got out of the canoe, and the next morning early I entered the church for service. The Rev. Thomas Vincent, who has built both his house and church, principally with his own hands, is most indefatigable. I saw no heathen Indians here, I heard no Indian drums, I beheld no superstitious rites, but I heard hymns of praise rising to heaven. A large number had been prepared for confirmation, and many knelt at the Lord's table.'

After a stay of a fortnight's duration the bishop returned to Moose, and started for Matawakumma, 500 miles distant, where the Rev. John Saunders, a native, like Mr. Vincent, of Albany, was now located. Matawakumma means, 'the lake of the meeting of the waters.' It is a large lake, irregular in outline, surrounded by woods. The first thing which strikes the visitor on approaching the station is the neat little church perched on a rising ground, like a beacon set on a hill, the rallying point for the little band of Ojibbeway

Indians of the neighbourhood. Then the residence of the fur-trader comes in sight, the store and other buildings, and the modest parsonage-house, with its garden and accessories. The whole way from Moose the bishop saw not more than a dozen people. The journey took rather more than a fortnight. The road was a broad river, impeded in its course by many rapids and shoals, and by numerous waterfalls, some of which are very beautiful.

'Various portages had been made, and we were going on, as we thought, safely,' writes the bishop, 'when suddenly there is a heavy crash, and the water comes rushing into the canoe. We had come with force upon a rock, which had made a great hole in the bark. We paddle to the shore as fast as possible, take everything out of the canoe and begin repairing it. One goes to a birch tree and cuts off a large piece of bark, another digs up some roots and splits them, a third prepares some pitch, and in the course of an hour or two the bark is sewn into the bottom of the canoe, the seams are covered with pitch, and we are once more loading our little vessel.

'At the end of our second week we come to an encampment of Indians. It is Sunday, and we stay and spend the day with them. They are old friends, Henry Martyn and his wife and others. Indians who are Christians, baptized and communicants. Indians who can give a reason for the hope which is in them. Indians who can read their books and write their letters, and who may be depended upon quite as much as any Europeans.

SHOOTING A RAPID

'Early on Monday morning we are once more in our canoe, and soon get into Matawakumma Lake, in which we paddle for five hours in very heavy rain. Soaked quite through, we feel not a little glad to step ashore on the friendly beach, and find ourselves once more with civilised man.'

And ere long the time came for the bishop's sore trial of parting with wife and children. The two youngest must go to an English school. But 'who was to take them?' he writes. 'There was no one but their dear mother, and although it was hard to part with her in this dreary and solitary land, it was absolutely necessary; and they were to be accompanied by my eldest son, Dr. Horden, who had spent the winter with us. Our annual ship came early, and the party was to start in her on her return voyage. I spent one night on board. Next morning, at an early hour, the ship's guns told us that the voyage had commenced. I remained until after breakfast, and then, after a sorrowful farewell, I left in a boat, and in a few minutes found myself on the deck of the schooner bound for Fort George.

'Now the way to Fort George is, in part, the way to England, and so the two vessels started in company. The day was beautiful, the wind was fair, and we made good progress; but the great ship, spreading more canvas, gradually got ahead—late in the evening she was about twelve miles distant, and I thought we had seen the last of her. That night and the next day the weather was very wild and disagreeable, but the day, after all, was once more prosperous, and soon after breakfast we espied our huge companion a few miles to the west of us. She drew towards us, and when we saw the last of her, as night came on, she was about ten miles ahead.

'The following day we should easily have reached our destination had the weather been clear; as it was, we could not venture near the dangerous coast. On Sunday the weather cleared up, the high land of Wastekan Island came in sight, and by-and-by the low and dangerous lead islands. Then the wild and uninviting land all around showed we were at the mouth of Big River, the tortuous channel of which we carefully threaded, and at four o'clock we dropped anchor in front of the little village, consisting only of six or eight houses. .

'I was agreeably surprised to find a large number of my red friends assembled on the beach to greet me. I at once collected them together, and we had a most interesting service. Later in the evening we had the English-speaking people and the crew of our vessel, making altogether quite a respectable congregation. On Friday morning we had to say good-bye, and once more go on board. The next day was dark and dismal, the wind blowing a hurricane, while the sea ran mountains high. At noon we caught a momentary sight of land, but we were obliged to stand out, as we could not see our way through the tortuous course to Moose. No one on board slept a moment that night. The storm abated in the morning, and at daybreak we were once more sailing in the right direction; in the afternoon the wind was very light, and a little after six o'clock we landed at Moose. I made my way to my own house; the loved ones, who were accustomed to greet me with such joy on my return, were far away, battling with the great Atlantic waves. . . . They were gone, and it ill became me to sit down and mope; so I set to work to drive melancholy away. More work came upon me than I had calculated upon.

'This was the only winter that Mr. Saunders, the Ojibbeway clergyman, could be at Moose for a long time, and I could not translate into the Ojibbeway tongue without his assistance. We first attacked the Moosonee hymn-book. This finished, we commenced the Prayer-book, and having finished the morning prayers we put it aside to get one of the Gospels done. The great diversity of languages in the diocese vastly increases our labour—Cree, Ojibbeway, Chipwyan, and Eskimo—and there must be separate translations for each. The English school, too, I manage myself, with over thirty scholars. They are a happy lot, very well behaved, with a great love for their school—as a proof of which I need only say that there has been scarcely an absentee for the winter. All this, with sermons, visiting my people, correspondence, which grows instead of diminishing, keeps me thoroughly employed every day from morning to night. The winter hitherto has been a very mild one. When it stands at or a little above zero, we consider it decidedly warm.

'Of all I received last ship time nothing gladdened my eyes more than the sight of a box of Eskimo books in the syllabic character, printed from manuscript sent home the previous year. I can fancy with what delight Mr. Peck pounced on them, and with what gratification the Eskimo beheld the raising of the lid which exposed to view so much spiritual food. Our native library is becoming extensive, new books being added every year. There is no language without literature. It is blessed work supplying the aborigines of any country with the Word of Life; that Word which reveals to them Jesus, and raises them in spiritual things to a level with the most polished and civilised nations on earth.'

CHAPTER XIII

YORK FACTORY

LEAVING the station in charge of the Rev. J. Keen, the bishop started, in June 1879, on the long contemplated visit to York Factory, in the northern part of his diocese. 'I left Moose,' he says, 'or June 30, having made every necessary arrangement for the management of the mission during my absence. At Michipicoton, close to the mighty Lake Superior, kind friends were my hosts for four days, days full of work, and then a steamer carried me to Sault St. Marie, a long way out of my course, where I was obliged to remain a week, during which I was the guest of another missionary bishop, the Bishop of Algoma, whose diocese is rapidly filling up from England and the well-peopled parts of Canada.

'I went through Lake Superior. Four-and-twenty hours of railroad followed, and fourteen hours more of steamer, and the second stage was completed. A month was spent with my kind friend the Bishop of Rupertsland. I was in the centre of the civilisation of the country, in the neighbourhood of Winnipeg, only a few years ago a waste, now a populous town, with splendid schools, churches, banks, colleges, town hall, &c. I was constantly at work, preaching in the various churches, sometimes in Cree, sometimes in English, added to which to my lot fell the duty of preaching the sermon at the opening of the synod, at which the clergy were collected from various parts of the country. I need not say how thoroughly this month was enjoyed; it gave me the largest amount of Christian intercourse I have had for several years.

'When the steamer which was to convey me through Lake Winnipeg was ready to start I went on board, and in her had a journey of three hundred miles to Old Fort, from which I was conveyed to Norfolk House by boat. I was far enough away from civilisation now, and had before me five hundred miles of dreary and desolate country. There were some immense lakes to cross, and some rough rapids to descend; but we saw no bold falls, such as I have been accustomed to find in other parts of the country.

'On September 19 I found myself at my journey's end, at York Factory, a spot I had longed to visit for many, many years, a spot at which several devoted missionaries have laboured, where Christ has been faithfully preached, and where many precious souls have been gathered into His garner.'

The Rev. J. Winter had arrived at the station to take the place of Archdeacon Kirkby, who had quitted York by the annual ship just a week before. Mr. Winter had heard the archdeacon's farewell sermon. The latter had faithfully toiled there for twenty-seven years, and there was scarcely a dry eye. The interpreter was the first to break down, then followed the archdeacon himself, together with the congregation. For a few moments there was a pause; it was with difficulty that he finished his discourse. 'I had wished,' wrote the bishop, 'to express to him personally my sense of the praiseworthy manner in which he had, single-handed, managed this large district. It needs more labourers—one at Churchill, and another at Trout Lake. One great difficulty is the number of languages spoken. At York and Severn, Cree; at Trout Lake, a mixture of Cree and Saulteaux; and at Churchill, Chipwyan and Eskimo, which have no resemblance either to each other or to the Cree or Saulteaux. I have been busy ever since coming here, for besides the Indian there is a somewhat large English congregation, York having ever been a place of great importance in the country, although it is now much less so than formerly. I conduct an English school daily, give lessons in Cree to Mr. Winter, and twice a week I give lessons to the European and native servants of the Hudson's Bay Company. Altogether I am as fully employed as I have ever been at Moose; but I cannot but know that with me the sun has passed the meridian, and that it behoves one to work while it is called to-day.

'In January I go northward two hundred miles to Churchill, the most northerly inhabited spot in the diocese of Moosonee. It is a very dreary place. The wife of the gentleman in charge there, the sister of one of our missionaries, is often years without seeing the face of a civilised woman, while the intensity of the cold there is as great almost as in any spot on the earth's surface. You may conceive with what joy a visitor is received. What a welcome I may expect on my arrival! The Indians there will be quite strange to me; with their language I am not at all acquainted. I had never seen one until I came here, and here only one—a poor girl, now a happy, comfortable, Christian lassie, with an English tongue, but who was cast out as an encumbrance by her unnatural relatives. In June I go on a tour to Trout Lake and Severn; this will occupy me nearly two months, and in August I once more set off for England.'

The voyage from York Factory in the autumn of 1880 was the most tedious and stormy on record, occupying ten weeks instead of five. It was the middle of November ere Bishop Horden reached England, when once more he had the joy of greeting his wife and children. And now followed a continual round of preaching, speaking, and travelling, with very heavy daily correspondence. At many a meeting the bishop held his audience in rapt attention with the story of the rise and progress of the Moose mission, with graphic descriptions of parts of the Moose diocese, with accounts of the work in the six several districts into which it was now divided, each under the care of an ordained clergyman. Charters had been granted to two companies for the construction of railways from the corn-growing provinces of Manitoba and Saskatchewan to the shores of Hudson's Bay, one or both of which would run for the greater part through the Moosonee diocese. The bishop pleaded for help, therefore, for a church extension fund. He would often close his address with an Indian's account of the condition of his people when in a state of heathenism, giving it in the native Cree, with a literal translation.

Naspich ne ke muchepimatisin wāskuch numa kākwan
Very I was bad formerly not anything
ne kiskāletān piko Muchemuneto ishpish ka primatiseyan ;
I know it only the devil as long as I lived
misew ā ililewuk ne ke wapumowuk moshuk ā muchepima-
all the Indians I saw them always they being
tisitchik, ā notenittochik, ā keshkwāpāchik,
wicked when they fight with each other when they get drunk
ā mukoshāchik, ā mitāwitchik, ā kosapatutik,
when they feast when they conjure when they pretend to prophesy
ā kelaskitchik ; muskumāö wewa, nutopowuk,
when they lie he takes from him by force his wife they ask for liquor
naspich, saketowuk, utawāwuk, kimotaskāwuk
much they like it they buy it they rob (other) people's lands
kisewahaö weche ililewa, naspich tapwā
he angers them his fellow Indians, very truly
ke muhepimatisewuk.
they were wicked.

These sentences will illustrate the peculiar structure of the Indian tongue, which, with its 'sesquipedalian compounds,' as Professor Max Müller calls them, might deter almost any student from the attempt to master it. Bishop Horden, with great patience, perseverance, and thoroughness, compiled a grammar of the Cree language, which appeared about this time, and in which we are, step by step, introduced to a system complete in the mechanism of all its parts. Words that seem all confusion gradually assume their proper forms. Around the verb, which is the most important factor in the formation of those polysyllabic words, cluster all the other ideas. They are glued on to it, so to speak. That which with us would be a whole sentence is accumulated in the Cree into a long compound word; agent, action, object, with adverbial expletives, are all combined.

The bishop, in the midst of all his hard work when in England, now speaking for the Church Missionary Society, now pleading for his own diocese, in the midst of engagements and travel, in the midst even of his very journeyings to and fro, found time to write some of his graphic descriptive papers. We give the following true story of one of the former Coral School children, written by him in the waiting-room of a railway station, whilst expecting a train.

'Amelia Davey was originally named Amelia Ward, and was one of the children of the Coral Fund. She got on with her learning very well, could read and write English creditably, and spoke English as well as if she had been an English girl, instead of a Cree. At the age of about nineteen she married a young Indian named James Okune Shesh; and, after about three years of married life, lost him through disease and starvation, she herself narrowly escaping death.

'Some time afterwards she married another Indian, named Solomon Davey, a good steady man, who was to her an excellent husband. Last autumn they left Moose Factory with their children, accompanied by Davey's old father and mother, for their winter hunting-grounds. For a time all went well, fish and rabbits supplying the daily needs of the family; the food gradually, however, failed, until scarcely any was obtainable. Day after day Solomon went off to seek supplies; evening after evening he returned bringing little or nothing. The party now determined to make their way to Moose; there they knew their wants would be relieved, but Solomon's strength entirely broke down, and they were obliged to place him on a sledge, which was hauled by his mother; thus they moved painfully forward. The poor fellow was covered up as well as possible. He seemed very quiet; his mother went to him to assure herself that all was right; but the spirit had fled. The brave good Indian, who had done his best to supply the wants of those dependent on him, had perished in the attempt. Fresh trouble came; Amelia's time had come for the arrival of another baby; camp was made, and a little unsuspecting mortal was ushered into the world.

'How they lived I know not; but two days after the child's birth, Amelia, tying up her little one, and placing it on her back, and putting her snow-shoes on her feet, essayed to walk to Moose, still eighteen miles distant. Bravely she stepped out; her own life as well as the lives of those she left behind depended on her reaching it. She slept once; the bitter cold seemed anxious to make her its victim, but the morning still beheld the thin spare form alive, and, asking God to give her the strength she so sorely needed, she struggled on again.

'Presently the houses of Moose make their appearance, but they are far, far off. Can they be reached? It seems scarcely possible, but the effort is made, the necessary strength is supplied, and she finds herself in a house, with Christian hands and Christian hearts to minister to her necessities.

'But can this poor wrinkled old woman, apparently sixty years of age, be the bright, well-favoured, cheerful Amelia of thirty? The very same. What you see has been produced by the cold and want; and how about the babe? Well, the dear little baby was well and strong; the Christian mother had preserved it with the greatest imaginable care, and it was to her, doubtless, all the more dear from the terrible circumstances under which it was born.

'Parties were at once sent off to those left behind, with food and other necessaries, and all were brought to Moose, where they were kindly and abundantly cared for. The last thing Solomon did last autumn was to go to the Rev. J. H. Keen, and purchase for himself a Cree New Testament to take with him to his hunting-grounds.'

Other stories the bishop told or wrote, too many for the size of the present volume. There was David Anderson, one of the many lambs of the Bishop of Rupertsland's flock, whose arm was shattered by an accidental gunshot, and for whom a false arm was sent out from England. This arm for a time he would not use, because he thought it wrong thus to supplement a limb of which 'God had seen fit to deprive him!' There was the devoted wife of the dying hunter (Jacob Matamashkum), who saved him in the last pangs of starvation by applying his lips to her own breast. There was the aged grandmother (good old Widow Charlotte), who took the dead daughter's babe and nourished it at her bosom thirty years after her own last child had been born. There was Richard, son of the Widow Charlotte, who was 'a famous fisherwoman' even after she had become a great grandmother. The son was a delicate young man, who had largely depended on her for subsistence. He married and fell ill. The poor wife on the morning before he died ruptured a blood-vessel in driving in a tent-peg, and was carried to the grave just a month after him. There were the starving parents, who, having lost their two youngest children from hunger, set off with the remaining two for the nearest station, a hundred miles away, to get food. The wife drew the sledge on which the children lay, while the husband walked in front to break a road in the snow for her, till at last his strength failed, and he could go no further. She, however, set up a little tent for him, and hastened on. She might yet get help in time to save him. She reached Albany, and sank unconscious. But friends were at hand—the children, scarcely alive, were taken from the sledge. The mother recovered to say where her husband lay. A party went in search of him; he was dead, and the body was hard frozen.

Many of the school-children wrote to the bishop

whilst he was in England letters, that might favourably compare with those of children possessing far greater advantages than they. All spoke of deepest attachment to him, all longed for his return amongst them. 'We shall be so happy to see you again,' was the refrain of every letter. The elder sister of one of the girls had become the wife of the Rev. J. Saunders, native pastor of Matawakumma. Her letter addressed to Mrs. Horden is full of interest. It is dated August 13, 1881. She says:

'We are pretty dull up here, but we enjoy good health, and we must feel thankful to Him who gives us health and life. Of course you know that we spent the first winter you were away at Moose, and I must say your absence was very much felt, and when the bishop went away the following summer, Moose was quite deserted.

'I think the people at Moose will be very glad to see you back again. Sometimes I wish to see Moose and my friends living there, but, knowing the difficulty and expense of travelling, I put the subject out of my mind, and try to feel contented. If this place was not such a poor one for living I should certainly feel more settled. In the winter we do very well in the way of food, but my husband is obliged to occupy a good deal of his time in hunting; but in the summer we depend altogether on our nets, and if fish fails, then there is nothing at all; but I am glad to say that it is only sometimes that we get only enough for breakfast. I feel happy to say that our Heavenly Father never allows us to be without food altogether, and we bless the Bounteous Hand which can give us food even in this bleak and lonely wilderness. Many times while I was at Moose I thought it would be impossible to exist on fish alone, but experience teaches me that we can exist on fish, and fish alone. Many times I think how nice and helpful it would be if we had a cow.

'I feel rather surprised that my husband did not arrange with the bishop before this to have a cow; to my mind that should have been considered before now. The other missionaries have cattle, and I think we could keep a cow very nicely here. I am afraid I shall be tiring you, so I must conclude my letter, wishing you and yours every blessing.

'I remain yours very gratefully,

'FRANCES SAUNDERS.'

The bishop did not return to Moose in the summer of 1881. He found much to do in England, and so the annual ship by which he was expected arrived without him. The Rev. Thomas Vincent visited Moose, taking the place of the Rev. J. Keen, in the course of the winter, which was a mild one. The summer had been dry, and there had been many forest fires—hundreds of young rabbits and partridges must have been roasted alive. A sad loss for the Indians, who largely depend on these for food.

CHAPTER XIV

THE RETURN TO MOOSE

IN the spring of 1882, the good folk at Moose became more and more pressing for their beloved bishop's return. They were looking eagerly forward to his presence amongst them again; and he went, but he went alone, Mrs. Horden remaining in England with their children. A fortnight after his arrival in Moose he wrote:

'My canoe journey occupied eighteen days, and was rather arduous. The heat, against which there could never be the slightest protection, was terrible, sometimes rising as high as 110° in the shade, which was aggravated by the rocky and difficult character of many of our portages. These things were nothing to me some years ago, but it is different now. I cannot bear fatigue as I could when I came by the same route fifteen years ago; then it was physically a pleasure, now it is a labour.'

The bishop had travelled *viâ* New York, Montreal and Matawa. 'We alighted at the station,' he writes, 'and a mile ride on a very rough road brought us to the thriving young town. Fifteen years ago, with wife and two young children, I had found the reaching

Matawa a difficult journey by canoe, and when I had reached it, it consisted of three houses; now its population is about five hundred, while the number of people passing through is very large. It has fine shops, many hotels, a broad street, and an English church and parsonage are being built for a very energetic resident clergyman. It is the seat of the lumber trade in the Upper Ottawa; hence its importance. But where are the Indians, who not long since were numerous here? This place knows them no more! I saw scarcely any; as a race they have passed away; many have died, for they cannot stand the diseases Europeans bring with them—measles, whooping-cough, diphtheria, make short work of them. Many, too, have gone to work on the railways, while the women have married French Canadians, and so the Indian becomes swallowed up by the advancing whites.

'I travelled on by rail as far as the railroad went—forty miles from Matawa. The country is rocky and uninteresting, with a good spot for farming here and there. This railroad forms part of the Great Canadian Pacific, which is being carried forward with extraordinary rapidity, and will be accomplished years before it was expected to be, the part causing most difficulty being that north of Lake Superior. At Matawa I remained four days, the guest of Mr. and Mrs. Bliss, spending a Sunday there, which I much enjoyed. I preached both morning and evening, and in the afternoon gave an address to the children. I never spend an idle Sunday. I should hope no one ever does; but a Sunday never passes without my saying something for the Master in a public manner. I feel that I must work; the truth comes home to me more and more forcibly every day that "the time is short," that it behoves us to work while it is called to-day.

'On Tuesday, August 1, I had done with railways and telegrams, almost with letters, and was once more in my birch-bark canoe up the Ottawa. There lies the bedding, tied up in an oil-cloth to prevent its getting wet; there the provisions, and the kettles and frying-pan, and tent and paddles; and here are my companions—four Temiscamingue Indians, fine strong fellows, who with alacrity place the canoe in the water, and then everything in it in a very orderly manner; then one of them with a respectful touch of his cap says, "*Ashi nen he posetonau kekinow*" ("Already we have embarked everything"). I step into the canoe; a nice seat has been prepared for me, and we are off. The sound of the paddles is familiar; I could almost forget that I had not heard it for two years. Through the whole course of our journey I did not see a dozen farms. But what is this I see? Logs, logs, logs; tens, hundreds, thousands, all formed into a raft, on their way to build houses, churches, palaces, cottages, in the civilised world. And here we are at the foot of a great rapid; we are obliged to get out of our canoe, which, with all the baggage, has to be carried over a long portage. But there comes a curious-looking structure, square in shape, and on it a couple of small houses and four men. It is composed

CANADIAN TIMBER

of a large number of squared logs formed into a small raft called a "crib"; the men look resolute and determined, and handle immense oars called sweeps. They come on towards the rapid, slowly at first, then the speed increases, and down they go, covered with water, down, down, down, until quieter waters are reached. A few more strokes of the oar send it out into mid-stream, where it will wait until all the other cribs have descended, when they will be again joined together, and so go on until the next rapid is reached. As we sit, crib after crib descends without accident; but it is dangerous work, and the Ottawa frequently secures its victims.

'We have a good deal of portaging, and very hot it is. On this portage there is an abundance of blueberries; we gather and eat them, and capitally they quench our thirst, almost making us forget the fiery sun above us. At the head of the Long Sault our difficulties are over, we are on the placid waters of the great Lake Temiscamingue. Some time after it has become quite dark, one of my companions exclaims, "*Ma!*" ("Listen") "*kagat iskota chemau*" ("truly the fire-boat"—the steamer); and in the distance I hear the puffing of the giant, who has now invaded these hitherto quiet waters. At midnight we put up our tent and seek repose; we set off again early, and about four P.M. reach Temiscamingue.

'Five days beyond Temiscamingue we found ourselves on the broad waters of the Abbitibbe Lake, a grand expanse, dotted with islands, which make it in places very picturesque. And there stands the

Hudson's Bay Company establishment, where I am sure of a welcome.'

A few days later the bishop landed at Long Portage House, a small and lonely establishment. All are friends here, and preparations are at once made for a service, which all greatly enjoy. 'And there is a beautiful little baby to baptize,' continues the child-loving bishop, and there are several who are anxious to receive the sacrament of the Lord's Supper.

'I wished to get to Moose before the ship, so before six o'clock we are in our canoe and hurrying forwards ; down we plunge over our last great rapid, and are in the Moose River. We are soon nearing Moose, and already come upon some of its people. Here is Widow Charlotte in her canoe, fishing ; her face brightens as she grasps my hand and tells me how thankful she is to see me once more ; she looks well, but the last three years have told greatly upon her. A little further on we meet stirring Widow Harriet, engaged in the same occupation. At breakfast-time we meet a large canoe on its way to Abbitibbe, containing a family returning to Canada ; we breakfast and have prayers together, and I learn that the ship arrived safely from England two days ago, and that all were well. We paddle on, pass the Bill of Portland, and the Mill, and the winter fishing-place at the mouth of Maidman's Creek, and we cross the broad river, and sweep round the head of Charles Island. Here is Sawpit Island, and there, directly in front of us, is Moose Island, but showing no signs of

MOOSE FACTORY, CAPITAL OF THE DIOCESE OF MOOSONEE

1, Bishop's Court; 2, school-house; 3, cottage (residence of a good helper); 4, cottage (residence of catechist); 5, stores; 6, church; 7, residence of chief factor; 8, residence of officers; 9, large store and sale shop; 10, cattle byres; 11, Pontypool, a mile below the church

being inhabited. We travel along it, we round its head, and a new world lies before us—for it seems indeed nothing less, coming as one does on the large thriving establishment after days of travel in the wilderness.'

Moose at this time and at this season presented an even still more pleasant aspect than when, some thirty years before, the Bishop of Rupertsland had described it as the prettiest spot in the country. Since then it has somewhat increased in importance, and the condition of the buildings and their surroundings give it a charming appearance.

The grazing cattle first attract attention, then the neat residence of the bishop and the other mission buildings, the adjoining cottages with their well-kept gardens, and a number of Indian tents and marquees in the foreground, the church with its metal covered spire glistening in the sun's rays a little distance off. Near the landing-place are the Hudson's Bay Company buildings, the substantial residence of the company's representative and that of his subordinate officers. The large handsome store, and a good garden, with the steward's house adjoining, with a group of workshops —carpenter's, joiner's, cooper's, and the blacksmith's forge behind, cow-houses and stables for cattle, horses, pigs, and sheep. In the foreground is the graveyard neatly fenced round; then a field of waving barley, another of potatoes, and a large hay-meadow, with again a group of cottages, gardens, and tents.

The ship had come in, and people were hurrying about everywhere. The Mink was receiving cargo, the Marten too, as well as a barge with sails set.

These transferred their contents to large flat-bottomed boats, which conveyed them to a store by the riverside. Along the banks were moored many smaller craft, full of grass, brought from the salt marshes, to be turned into hay for the cattle during the long winter. In the midst of all the bustle the advent of the bishop in his canoe is observed. The white mission flag is hastily run up. The red flag of the Hudson's Bay Company is hoisted. The mission party, which includes Archdeacon Vincent from Albany and Mr. Peck from Fort George, as well as two young missionaries, the Rev. H. Nevitt and Rev. J. Lofthouse, who had come by the ship, and Mrs. Saunders from Matawakumma, hasten to the landing-stage. The bishop's daughter Chrissie, with her husband, Mr. Broughton, and their three boys, Kelk, Fred and Arthur, are there already, and the first greetings are not given before the chief members of the station are all collected about the bishop. All are anxious to welcome him and to give him the news he longs to hear, of the welfare of themselves and the various members of his flock in the different parts of his diocese. Then the bell from the church tower sends forth its summons, and the Indians hurry to respond to it, and soon the church is filled from end to end by an eager and interested congregation. He to whom they all look as a father has come back, and having given their greeting and received his blessing, they depart again to their several occupations.

The bishop was speedily immersed in work. Only a few days after his return he confirmed forty-five young Indians, men and women who had been carefully prepared by Mr. Vincent. Later on he confirmed all the English-speaking young people, both half-caste and Indian. His heart was cheered by the progress made in the mission during his absence. The church was not large enough to contain the congregation. The winter came and passed.

The spring-tide of 1883 was not a cheerful one, and the bishop felt the contrast between the scene in his out-of-the-world home and the surroundings in which he had passed the preceding year. '*Mispoor, mispoor, mispoor*'—'Snow, snow, snow,' he wrote on May 2, 'everything white, the ground all covered, the river all dead and still—the ice-covering four feet thick. . . . I turned to my table and found comfort from reading a portion of the Book of books, God's great gift to mankind, until I was called to prayers. Family prayers they were, and yet no member of my family knelt with me; the nearest is a hundred miles distant, the rest thousands.'

Not until May 21 did the ice begin to break. 'On Trinity Sunday I looked out at three o'clock—all was still, and I lay down again. At five I once more looked out—the operation of breaking-up had commenced. In the evening the river, which for so many months had shown no signs of life, was rolling on in a vast flood.'

In the summer of this year whooping-cough once more broke out at Moose and Albany. At the latter place forty-four died of it; amongst the number the bishop's infant grandson. At Moose, the illness raged almost as fiercely. Day after day funerals are recorded by the bishop, who was much depressed by the mourning and sadness around him. 'Could I,' he says, 'when the service is over, come back to a cheerful home, it would be different, but I come back to the once joyous, but now solitary house, to hear my own footsteps, and to feed upon my own thoughts.'

On August 22 a terrible storm broke over Mocse. The morning dawned brightly, and everything betokened a beautiful summer day. The sun shone out, the air was warm, and the wind blew from the south-east. After breakfast the wind grew stronger and yet stronger, until it became a perfect hurricane. Forest trees bent like wands, some were torn up by the roots, others snapped in two. The river was like a tempest-tossed sea. The great flagstaff of the Hudson's Bay Company came down with a mighty crash. The mission flagstaff swayed to and fro, threatening every instant to fall. The houses suffered little, being built of solid logs, strongly bolted together with iron bolts. That Wednesday night was a fearful one, the next day not quite so bad. The weather continued dull and raining. The ship was expected, and a load of anxiety would be removed by its arrival. But September dawned, and there was no ship!

'It is now September 5, and one of the gloomiest days I have known for a very long time. The haycocks are lying in the fields, thoroughly drenched, and turning black from their long exposure to the daily downpour. The potatoes are cut down by the heavy frost of last Saturday, and the barley lies prostrate. All this we could bear, but this year there is a fear that we may have to depend more on what our fields may give than is generally the case, for as yet there is no ship. We have had a vessel lying at the river's mouth for nearly a month waiting for her, and every face begins to look serious. There is good cause, for there are not sufficient supplies here for another year. Of wine there is none. Of medicine, scarcely any. A restriction has been put on the sale of food and clothing; the supply is scanty, and the look-out is really very dark indeed. What adds so much to our gloom is the saddening fact that death is still amongst us, carrying off our little ones amid great suffering.'

The 7th of September passed, but the joyful cry of 'The ship is come!' had not been raised. The hearts of the watchers began to grow sick with hope deferred, and all sorts of conjectures were formed as to the cause of the delay. On September 10 the bishop wrote, 'Our gloom deepens as day succeeds day, and we get no tidings of our ship. There are parties here from distant stations all waiting, but in a couple of days all must leave, so as to burden us no longer for the provisions they require. September 15. Our ship has not come, and I am afraid now it will not come. You can have no idea of our state of anxiety. She may come yet, and I trust she may; but it is now so late that we are beginning to give up hope. And here we are, with no medicine or wine for the sick, scarcely any candles, a very limited supply of tea and sugar, a very scanty supply of clothing, only half a crop of potatoes, and no hope of improvement for nearly twelve months. I feel that we must not run these risks in future. It is absolutely necessary that we should have at Moose a full year's supply for all our missions in this quarter. It *must be done*,[1] and I shall require 500*l*., which will be expended in the purchase of flour, tea, sugar, salt pork, bacon, preserved Australian beef, &c. We shall then always have a year's stock of necessaries on hand, and so be independent for one year of the ship's arrival.'

At last, when all hope had fled from the breasts of those who so long had watched, and watched in vain, on the morning of September 21 the cry was raised, 'The ship's come!' 'Magic words,' the bishop wrote, 'which entirely changed the current of our thoughts.'

The flag was hoisted to announce the event, and everyone was full of grateful joy, everyone busy with a helping hand, for the weather was already winterly, with snow falling every day, and the ship must start quickly on her return voyage. The danger was that she might not reach home again in safety so late in the season. She had been delayed for weeks in the ice in coming out, and the return voyage was indeed a terrible one. The water in the ship's tanks froze some inches thick, and heavy gales and blinding snow-storms accompanied her until she reached England late in November.

Moosonee has two ports, Moose Factory and York

[1] It was done by the Coral Fund.

Factory, and the York ship that year could not return to England at all. She had arrived at York when the people were almost in despair, and had then set out for Churchill, where she was weather-bound. This place is so small and out of the world, that as soon as possible the crew was transferred to York Factory, where there was better accommodation for them, the men having to walk thither two hundred miles on snow-shoes.

CHAPTER XV

TRYING TIMES

THE summer of 1884 was again a sickly one ; a severe influenza cold attacked almost everyone. The bishop had accomplished two visitation tours, when a cry of distress came from Albany. The sickness was there; many in the prime of life were dying. Archdeacon Vincent was himself ill. The bishop went. Morning, noon and night he was by the bedside of the sufferers, or making up medicines for them, till at length a change took place ; and after a stay of four or five weeks he was able to return to Moose, taking with him Mr. Vincent and his eldest daughter.

It was September, and he was at once plunged in a whirl of business, for the battered old ship had come again, and it had brought so many fine packages of eatables and necessaries that every spare foot of the mission premises was filled with them.

The ship was again nearly a month behind her time. For a thousand miles she had contended with ice, and had been very severely handled. After she had sailed on her return voyage the various autumn works were rapidly proceeded with : garden produce was taken up ; the cattle and byres were made snug and taut; and for house and school 120 cords of wood were cut. Then the Indians, who had spent three or four months at the station, began to disperse, to shoot the geese and ducks so plentiful at that season, and to hunt the fur-bearing animals, which had by this time donned their valuable winter coats.

All are anxious to get to their winter quarters whilst the river is available for the canoes. They assemble for a last Sunday service at the station; family after family come to receive the bishop's parting words of counsel and advice; then the farewell is spoken. 'Farewell,' they say; 'we will not forget.' The last shake of the hand is given, and they go to their homes in the wilderness, not to return until the spring, unless some adverse or untoward circumstance compels them to come in.

Winter came. It set in severely, and much earlier than usual, preventing the fall fishery, much depended upon for the supply of winter food. All the more thankful was the bishop for the founding of the Moose store.

In January he wrote: 'It is a very great relief to know that the food is here. As to the store being put up, that must bide its time. Every person has as much as he can do, myself included. Just now wood and fire take precedence of everything else. Day after day chopping and hauling are going on, while the disappearance of our immense piles of wood tells pretty plainly of the difficulty we have in keeping up the necessary warmth in our houses.'

The past year had been a very chequered one,

outwardly full of trouble, bad seasons, unprecedented storms, fatal epidemics, cases of starvation, much to discourage and depress. Yet the bishop could write thankfully that he had been enabled to labour so continuously in this inclement and isolated land, he and his faithful band of assistants having visited nearly the whole of the great diocese in the course of the year. Everywhere the Gospel was received with readiness. 'We have now no active opposition,' he says; 'indeed, there are very few persons in the diocese, except those in the far north, who have not been baptized, by far the greater part into our own beloved Church. For those on the north-western part of the bay a man admirably adapted for the work has been appointed in the person of the Rev. J. Lofthouse, who longs, with God's blessing, to gather into Christ's fold the Eskimo of that region, as the Rev. E. J. Peck has done on the eastern side of the bay.

'For the present winter Mr. Lofthouse is at York Factory, in the place of Mr. Winter, who is in England on account of his wife's health; but I expect them back in the summer, when Mr. Lofthouse will go to his more northern home.'

The Rev. E. J. Peck visited Fort George and Great Whale River, and started from Little Whale River for the distant station of Ungava, at the entrance of the Hudson's Straits, to see the Indians and Eskimo of that quarter. He was then to embark on board the Hudson's Bay Company's steamer for Quebec, whence he was to proceed to England.

'The Rev. H. Nevitt remained at Moose all the summer, conducting services and school, and attending to the numerous needs of our large summer population.

'As soon as the river broke up, I set off for Long Portage House, a station one hundred and twenty miles distant, on the way to Canada. The Indians there are Ojibbeways, and as yet have not made much progress in the religious life; but they received my message with attention, and I trust will yet become emancipated from the superstitions which oppress them. Returning from Long Portage House, I remained a short time at Moose, and, making all necessary arrangements, went in my mission boat to Rupert's House, which I formerly visited yearly, and where I have long wished to see a missionary permanently settled, and for which I had too fondly hoped to see one arrive from England last autumn.

'Sad troubles have come upon my much loved people there during the last few years, numbers of them having died of starvation from the failure of deer, which were formerly very numerous in their hunting-grounds. I trust that such stories of misery and death as I was constrained to listen to will never fall on my ears again. My mission was very successful, for I was enabled not only to minister to all the Rupert's House Indians and residents, but likewise to the Indians of the far interior, who came in the different trading brigades from Mistasinnee, Waswanepe, Machiskun, and Nitchekwun. These are all Christians, many of them communicants, and the greater part of them read and write the syllabic characters very well. Rupert's House is a great centre of trade, hence the vital necessity of the establishment of a strong mission there.'

In returning from Rupert's House on a former occasion, somewhat late in the cold season, the bishop very nearly lost his life. He set off in a cariole, with a train of dogs, accompanied by two young Indians, travelling by night, to escape the danger of snow blindness from the glare of the sun on the snow. They crossed Rupert's Bay, and at Cabbages Willows took breakfast with an Indian woman whose husband was goose-hunting. After resting some hours they went on to the east point of Hannah Bay, intending to cross that night, but the air had become warm, and rain indicated a possible breaking up of the ice, so they reluctantly turned into the woods and encamped. In the morning the weather was again cold with a strong wind, so on they went. When they had reached the middle of the bay, about ten miles from the nearest land, the guide suddenly exclaimed:

'What is this! the tide is coming in, and the ice is breaking up.'

They looked seaward, and saw mass after mass rise up on end and fall again. The guide had a small stick in his hand; he struck the ice on which they were standing, and it went through; clearly there was but a step between them and death.

'Get into the cariole at once!' cried he, 'and let us hurry back. We may be saved yet!'

The bishop did so, and almost instantly the hinder

part of the cariole went through the ice into the sea. Faces blanched a little, but happily the dogs seemed aware of the danger and made no halt, but hurried onward as fast as they could go; there was no stoppage for a moment.

Running by the side of the cariole, one of his companions said to the bishop:

'Perhaps God is not pleased at your leaving the Indians so soon. Should we get back safely, the Indians will be very glad to see you again, for they are not tired of the teaching you gave them.'

In the afternoon they came to the Indian hut before alluded to. It was full now; several hunters were there, and geese were abundant. They were made very welcome, and sitting round the fire, all listened with wrapt attention to the guide as he narrated the incidents of the day. When he had finished they expressed their wonder and joy at the escape.

'Not long afterwards,' says the bishop; 'I went out to have a look at our surroundings. I soon came upon a curious sight: a high cross-like erection with lines attached to it covered with bones of animals and birds, and pieces of red and blue cloth and other things. I had never seen anything of the kind before, and had no idea what it was intended for. I called Wiskechan, the proprietor of the tent, and said, "What is this?"

'"Oh," said he, "this is my *mistikokan* (conjuring pole), which I shake in this way when I do my conjuring."

'Looking solemnly at him, I replied, "I have come to tell you of better things, of God's willingness to give you all things through Jesus Christ, His Son. If you wish to accept the message I have brought, you must give up this."

'Without a moment's hesitation he called for his axe, and instantly chopped the pole down. What a glorious end to a day of danger! My thanksgivings that night were very hearty. I slept in peace, surrounded by my red-skin brethren, and a little after the next noontide was again at Rupert's House.'

Rupert's House, which is called after Prince Rupert, cousin of King Charles II., to whom and a band of associates the king granted a charter, giving them exclusive rights to trade with the inhabitants of Hudson's Bay, is situated near the mouth of Rupert's River, which empties itself into the beautiful Hudson's Bay, studded with picturesque islands. It lies one hundred miles east of Moose, from which it is reached by a sea voyage in summer along the southern shore of Hudson's Bay, and by a snow-shoe or cariole journey in winter.

As a fur-trading post it is of considerable importance, being the head-quarters of a large district.

The posts dependent on it are East Main, Mistasinnee, Waswanepe, Nitchekwun, and Machiskun; and every summer large canoes come from each of those places, bringing all the furs collected during the previous twelve months, and taking back with them full loads of bags of flour, chests of tea, casks of sugar, bales of cloth, kegs of gunpowder, shot, cases of guns, and all the other etceteras which comprise an Indian's wants. The furs are examined, counted and sorted, made up into large bales, shipped on board the Moose schooner, and taken to Moose, where they remain until they are put on board the yearly ship, to be transported to England.

At Rupert's House the number of residents in the service of the Hudson's Bay Company was about fifty; these were all half-castes, but speaking English as well as if born in England. They were very well conducted, several of them were communicants; 'and although there is not yet, I am sorry to say,' wrote the bishop at that time, 'a resident clergyman among them, all are punctual in their attendance at an English service held for them by their trader every Sunday.

'The Indians did number somewhat over three hundred, but for the last few years they have suffered greatly from a failure of food. And many of them have been starved to death. All are now Christians, but when I first went to them they were in a sad state of heathenism; their minds were very dark, and their deeds corresponded thereto. They were devoted to conjuring, having the most superstitious dread of the conjurer's power. Their sick they never burdened themselves with for any length of time; there was the unfailing remedy of relief, the bowstring; for death required no attention save the burying of the body. Parents, as soon as they became dependent on their children, were subjected to the same operation.

Murder for gain was rife; indeed, I could hardly point to any place better adapted to illustrate the text, "The dark places of the earth are full of the habitations of cruelty," than Rupert's House. But of many of the Indians it might now be said, "But ye are washed, but ye are sanctified." All are baptized.

'In consequence of the immensity of my charge, I am not able to visit Rupert's House as I did formerly every summer. When my canoe was seen approaching, every man, woman, and child would leave their tents, and come and stand on the river's bank to see their "father," as they called me, and, if possible, to get a shake of his hand. For some years we had no church, but assembled in a large upper room kindly placed at our disposal. Within a short time of my arrival, it was always packed as full as it could hold, and so it would be two or three times every day of my stay. And then every family came to me privately, and we talked over the events of the previous winter: how they had been off for food; whether furs had been plentiful or not; who had been sick, and who had died; how they had followed their religious duties; what instruction they had given their children. The whole family history of the year was gone through, and reproof, commendation, or encouragement given, as the case required.

'How full of work was every day, and every minute of every day! From six o'clock in the morning until nearly nine at night, except at meal times, it was work, work, work; but what blessed work! How the people responded to every call! It was work which made me bless God for calling me to enjoy so high a privilege. And many see things now with a much clearer eye than when they were ministered to by His servant. He directed them to the Master, and into the Master's presence they have entered.'

The bishop was more and more desirous to be able to place a missionary permanently at Rupert's House. The Rev. H. Nevitt, who had already made acquaintance with the station, would have liked to be located there, but he could not be spared from Moose until someone came to take his place. The 'someone' expected had not come out in the last year's ship, and was still anxiously looked for.

In July the bishop visited Martin's Falls, a canoe voyage of three hundred miles from Albany. The Indians here he found not very satisfactory, being steeped much more deeply in heathenism than any others in the diocese, not very accessible, remaining at the station no longer than was necessary for their trading purposes. He determined to place a resident catechist there. He then went on two hundred and fifty miles further, by a most difficult route, to Osnaburgh, situated on a large and beautiful lake. Here, morning, noon, and night, the teaching went on. The bishop's heart was gladdened to see that God was blessing the work, and he made up his mind to appoint one of his divinity students as pastor at the post; in the meantime he left a trusty native agent, himself an Osnaburgh Indian, in charge.

In 1886 this man writes as follows:

'I wish to tell you I am doing the work you wanted me to do. Only some of the Osnaburgh Indians listen to me. I am always going about. Last fall I went very far to see the Cranes; they are good people, and say prayers morning and evening. I wish you would let Queen Victoria know that I am teaching her people to serve and fear God and to love Jesus.

'JAMES UMBASI.'

In July the Rev. J. Peck returned from his visit to England, bringing with him a wife. They remained for the time with the bishop. The Moose Church, or Cathedral, had been enlarged by means of a new chancel; the hundred seats thereby gained were a great comfort to the congregation. 'It is a long time,' says the bishop, 'since I felt happier than on the dedication day.'

Ship time was again approaching, not quite so anxious a time, now that a year's provision in advance was safely stored on the mission premises. The poor would not want, and the missionary would be fed. But how little did any think how greatly those stores would be needed this year!

The ship, the Princess Royal, came; she discharged her precious cargo, consisting of all the necessaries for all the inhabitants of South Moosonee; and then she reloaded with bales of furs, huge bags of feathers, and hogsheads of oil. She left her anchorage, and got out over the long and crooked bar at the mouth of the river. She was then assailed by a terrible storm of three days' duration, which drove her back over the bar again, and ashore on an extensive sand-bank. Here she was fiercely buffeted by the sea, and threatened to part asunder. The life-boat was lowered, and into it got the pilot, the second mate, and ten of the crew, who succeeded in reaching the schooner Martin, which lay at anchor in the river.

The captain and remainder of the crew were to follow in the pinnace, but the risk for the pinnace was greater than that for the life-boat, therefore they decided on remaining by the ship. The vessel was half full of water, and after a night of anxious watching they were taken ashore by the Martin. The vessel lay a total wreck about fourteen miles from Moose.

All was done that could be done for the ship-wrecked mariners. The men were taken into the employ of the Hudson's Bay Company, one of the carpenter's shops being fitted up for their accommodation. Their own cook prepared their meals. Mr. Peck was appointed chaplain to them, his sailor experiences especially fitting him for the service. The bishop and his divinity students held night-school for them twice a week, teaching navigation, reading, writing, and arithmetic, closing always with singing and study of the Scriptures and prayer.

All behaved well; the captain set his men an excellent example, never being absent from his place in church as long as he remained at the station.

In the midst of all this, the bishop was still occupied in his important translation work. He had in the summer examined and revised an edition of the *Pilgrim's Progress* into Cree, by the Rev. J. Vincent.

He hoped to be able to send the work home by the next ship, to be printed. The names of some of the characters in this work are remarkable for their length in the Cree dress. Christian is the same as in English, but Hopeful is Opuhosalems; Faithful is Atapwawinewen; Little Faith, Tapwayaletumowineshish; Evangelist is Miloachemowililew; Save-all is Misewamunachetow; Money-love is Sakeskooleanas; Worldly Wisdom is Uskewekutatawaletumowilileu! 'I think,' says the bishop, commenting on the translation, 'that the Indians of Moosonee will be as well able to appreciate and enjoy this wondrous book as the generality of their English brethren.' The work was printed with the help and through the agency of the Religious Tract Society (the friend and helper of all evangelical workers); and we give a specimen of it, that our readers may see what the printed page is like.

In March 1885, the bishop had at last been able to commence the erection of a new and large building in which to place the winter stores.

'We have been logging,' he wrote; 'I have two men and a boy cutting logs, and sawing them with large pit saws. They are working at Maidman Island, three miles distant. We shall not be able to get our boards home until open water, but when

ᒫᑲ ᐌᒋ ᓈᑕᒫᓇ ᓀᒪ ᐃᐡᐚᑌᒻ, ᐊᐧᐋᔨᑌ ᑭᒋ ᑭᔅᑭᓄᐊᒫᑲ-
ᐑᔮᓇ ᑫ ᐃᔑ ᒥᔅᑳᒫᓇ ᐱᒫᒋᐃᐧᐁᐃᐧᓇ× **ᐁ**ᑯ ᑳ ᐃᐧᑌᐟ, ᑭ
ᑲ ᐚᐸᑎᓯᑎᓇ ᐊᐧᐋᔨᑌ ᐁ ᒥᐧᓭᔑᒃ ᒉᔅᑲᓇᐤ, ᐁᑳ ᑳ ᐋᓯᒪᐠ,
ᒌᐱᔅᑯᐠ ᓀᒪ ᑯᑕᒃ ᑳ ᑭ ᑭᔅᑭᓄᑕᐃᔦᐸᓇ× ᐊᓂᒪ ᒉᔅᑲᓇᐤ, ᑭ
ᐃᐧᑌᐤ, ᑭ ᑲ ᑭᔅᑭᓄᐃᐧᓯᑯᓇ ᑫ ᐃᔑ ᓈᑕᒫᐟ ᐅᑭᒫᐤ ᐃᐧᑭ ᑳ
ᐋᔮᐟ ᑲᑫᒌᐧᐁᓯᑕᒍᐃᐧᐃᓂᓯᐤ ᑭᒋ ᒪᓂᓇᒃ ᐆᐅ ᒍᐃᐧ ᐃᐧᐊᐧᔑᐃᐧᓇ×
ᐁᑯ ᑎᔫᐯᑕᐧᐊᒃ, ᓂ ᑭ ᐸᔅᑲᓇ ᒫᑲ ᐆᑌ ᐃᔑ, ᐃᐧᐸᐦ ᑭᒋ
ᐌᐱᓇᒫᓇ ᑳ ᐃᐧᐊᐧᔑᔫᓇ× ᐃᔅᐱ ᒫᑲ ᐆᑕ ᑲ ᐅᑎᑕᒫᓇ ᓀᐢᑕ
ᐃᐧᔫᐸᑕᒫᓇ ᐁ ᐃᔑᓈᐧᑲᑭ ᑫᐧᑲᓇ, ᓂ ᑭ ᑭᐱᒋᓇ ᐁ ᓴᑭᔨᔫᓇ
ᒫᑲ ᓇᒪᐃᐧᓴ ᐁᑯ ᓂ ᑭᔅᑫᓯᑌᓇ ᒌᓂ ᑫ ᑐᑕᒫᓇ×

ᐁᑯ ᑳ ᐃᐧᑌᐟ ᒥᓘᐋᒋᒎᐃᓯᓯᐤ, ᐱᑕᒫ ᑲᔫᒥᑲᐸᐧᐃ ᑭ ᑲ
ᐚᐸᑎᓯᑎᓇ ᑭᒋᒪᓂᒎ ᐅᐟ ᐊᔪᒥᐃᐧᓇ× ᐁᑯ ᓈᐸᐃᐧᐟ ᐁ ᓇᓂ-
ᑭᐸᓯᐟ× ᑭ ᐃᑎᑯ ᒫᑲ, "ᔫᐧᑲ ᐁᑳ ᐋᑕᐁᓯᒥᒃ ᐊᓇ ᑳ
ᐋᔪᒥᐟ,' ᐌᓴ ᑭᐡᐱᓇ ᐁᑲ ᑭ ᐱᒫᒋᐅᒋᒃ ᐊᓂᑭ ᑲ ᑭ ᐋᑕᐧᐁ-
ᓯᒫᒋᒃ ᐊᓂᐃ ᑲ ᑭ ᐋᔪᒥᓯᒋ ᐆᑕ ᐊᔅᑭᒃ, ᐚᐃᐦ ᓇᒪᐃᐧᓴ
ᑭᓵᓈᐤ ᑭ ᑲ ᐱᒫᒋᐅᓈᓇᐤ, ᑭᐡᐱᓇ ᐃᑲᑌᓂᑌᔾᔅᑕᐧᐊᒃ ᐊᓇ
ᑭᒋᑭᔑᑯᒃ ᑳ ᐅᒋ ᐋᔪᒥᐟ." "ᐃᐯᕈᐧᐊ 12. 25. ᒥᓇ ᑭ
ᐃᐧᑌᐤ, "ᑳ ᐧᑲᔪᔅᑭᑎᒋᒃ ᒫᑲ ᒌᐧᐯᓭᓯᑕᒍᐃᐧᐃᓇ ᑲᑕ ᐅᒋ ᐱᒫᑎ-
ᓯᐊᐧᐠ; ᒫᑲ ᑭᐡᐱᓇ ᐊᐧᐁᓇ ᐃᓯᓯᐤ ᐊᔦᑲᐸᐃᐧᑌ, ᓇᒪᐃᐧᓴ
ᑲᑕ ᓅᐯᓯᒥᑯ ᓂᐟ ᐊᒑᐧᑲ" "ᐃᐯᕈᐧᐊ 10. 38. ᐆᒪ ᐊᔨᒋ
ᑭ ᐃᑌᐤ; ᑭᓴ ᐁᐧᐊᑯ ᑳ ᓈᑕᒫᓇ ᓇᓃᑳᑌᓯᑕᒍᐃᐧᐃᓇ; ᑭ ᑭ ᒫᒋ
ᐋᑕᐧᐁᓯᑕᐧᒫᓇ ᐅᑲᑫᔅᑫᐧᐃᓇ ᒥᔫᐧᐋᒋ ᑫᔅᑎᔨᐟ, ᓀᐢᑕ ᑭ ᑭ ᐊᑎ ᓇᑲ-
ᑌᓇ ᑲᔫᒉᓯᑕᒍᐃᐧ ᒉᔅᑲᓇᐤ, ᐚᐧᐋᐤ ᑫᑳᐟ ᐁ ᑭ ᓂᔑᐧᐊᓈᒋᐅᔦᓇ×

ᐁᑯ ᑲᑎᔅᑎᔦᓇ ᑳ ᐸᑭᔑᒃ ᐅᓯᑎᓯᒃ ᒌᐱᔅᑯᐠ ᐁ ᓂᐱᐟ, ᐁ
ᑌᐧᐯᐟ, "ᓂ ᑲᐧᑳᑕᑭᔨᓯᓐ; ᐌᓴ ᓂᔭ ᓂᔑᐧᐊᓈᒋᐅᔦᓇ." ᐁ ᐚᐸᑕᒃ

A PAGE OF THE CREE 'PILGRIM'S PROGRESS'

the sawing is completed we shall get on with the frame.'

April brought with it a second epidemic of influenza; the packeters returning from Abbitibbe with the letters conveyed it to Moose. Everyone, except a few Europeans, was attacked, and work was at a standstill. Many deaths resulted, and the bishop's heart was sad. The poor folks at Moose had been disappointed too by the failure of grey geese and wavies, as well as the beautiful snow-buntings, which generally come in clouds, just before the geese. The bishop greatly feared that when the Indians came in from their hunting-grounds they would all take the dreaded influenza, and that their tents would become the scene of disease and misery.

On May 8 the great guns, the break-up signal, were fired. The Indians follow the ice down, and so as soon as the passage was practicable canoe after canoe appeared opposite Bishop's Court, and the bank was alive with men, women, children, and dogs. 'There they were,' says the bishop, 'just as well as when they went in the autumn. We soon entered the house of prayer to thank our Heavenly Father for the loving care He had exercised towards those who for so many months had had their home amongst the gloomy forests of Moosonee. Each family was then seen apart, and I was made acquainted with the whole history of the winter.

'In June a dispersion took place, when most of the men manned the boats which take the supplies to the stations in the interior, and most of their wives and families going off to the fishing-stations, only to come in on Saturday to take part in the Sunday services. The morning of departure presented a busy scene—from the store issued the men, carrying bags of flour, kegs of pork and gunpowder, bales of cloth, calico, and leather, cases of guns, chests of tea, and all the things mentioned in a trader's inventory. All is snugly packed in the boats, the signal given, and they push off from the launch. It is a pretty sight, the men are all standing up, and their long iron-clad poles for a time rise together as they force their respective boats forward, bending to the work, and putting forth their strength.

'Two of the boats were under the guidance of Jacob Mekwatch, "our prince of hunters." The other three boats were under the charge of James Gideon, another excellent Indian and good hunter, who had several men among his crews who could conduct a service and deliver a very good address—for all of the most intelligent Indians are trained to do this, so that when there is no clergyman at the place one of them may be able to lead his fellow Indians in worship. All looked well, no one complained. But many days had not elapsed before influenza attacked the boats' crews; one after the other of the poor men succumbed, and was brought back to be under medical care. James Gideon became so ill that it was feared he would die, and many of his crew were but little better. It was a sad time, for many were taken ill so far up the river that it was judged best for them to remain with the boats. Happily, though there was so much sickness, there were no deaths. It was a sad, sad time.'

But brighter days dawned at last. Entrusting the station to Mr. Nevitt's care, the bishop started on a long visitation tour, from which he did not return till late in the autumn.

CHAPTER XVI

CHRISTMAS AND NEW YEAR'S DAY AT ALBANY

THE bishop was very busy during the early part of the winter of 1885, fulfilling the duties of the doctor (who was absent at Albany) in addition to his own. But he felt well and strong, and happy in the progress of all his work. He was revising and correcting his translation, with a view to a new edition being printed, of the Book of Common Prayer, and the hymn-book, which he had compiled many years before. The first editions of both he had himself printed at Moose, and bound too. In earlier days the Indians had carried their few pages of neatly written-out texts, and hymns, and Gospel portions between strips of bark fastened together with thongs of deer-skin. The first bound books were a strange novelty to them.

December found him once more setting out for Albany. The archdeacon having gone to England to see his *Pilgrim's Progress* through the press, the bishop had arranged to spend Christmas at that station. On December 18 he walked down to the starting-point. The sledge was already on the ice, and presently the dogs, each held by its own trace, were brought down

A DOG SLEDGE

and fastened to it—it being strongly moored the while, lest they should run off with it, so eager were they to go.

'All being ready, I got into my sledge and looked at my team. It was composed of twelve splendid creatures, perfectly clean, and in the best of order, with ears erect and their fine tails gracefully turned up over their backs; they were jumping and howling, endeavouring to move the sledge. I said good-bye to the numerous friends around me; I waved adieu to many others standing on the river's bank; the binding rope was cast off, and then not a sound was heard, save the soft movement of the sledge over the snow, and the tinkling of the musical bells attached to the dogs' necks. We sped down the river at a great rate; the houses were soon left behind, and we were in the wilderness. At the river's mouth the ice became quite smooth, with the smallest sprinkling of snow on its surface—its best possible condition. There was no cold in the air, I needed no wrapping up; it was the perfection of travelling. At about fourteen miles from Moose we saw the ill-fated Princess Royal, standing with her masts erect; a few miles further on, at the North Bluff Beacon, we remained for half an hour to give the dogs a rest, and to take a little refreshment. Then on and on; the dogs, requiring no whip to urge them, either galloped or went at a fast trot the whole way to Piskwamisk, "The place of the stone heaps," where we encamped. We had gone nearly forty miles in six hours. We soon made ourselves comfortable; a fire was lit in the tent, the robes spread, and in a little while a good cup of coffee was ready, which, with a biscuit, was enough until the evening's substantial meal.

'The good dogs were then attended to, the harness taken off, a collar with a chain attached was placed around each dog's neck, and, to prevent their indulging in the much-desired fight, each was fastened to a separate tree stump, close to which was strewn some fine brush for a bed. All were then served with a good supper of fish, and after looking round to see that no more was forthcoming, they coiled themselves up, with their tails over their heads, and nothing was heard of them until next morning. The whole of the next day we were obliged to remain in camp, the weather being very rough, and the atmosphere so thick that we could scarcely see fifty yards out to sea. It was still somewhat thick on the morning of the third day, but as meat for the dogs failed we were obliged to proceed. It cleared soon after starting, and four hours brought us to our next encampment, Cock Point. We were now forty miles from Albany, and this we accomplished in little more than six hours on the day following.

'I found all well: young Kelk and his brothers quite as ready for a romp as ever, and as ready as ever to run a snow-shoe race, or join in the glorious game of "tobogganing." But work was to occupy most of my attention. I visited all the people, by whom I was most warmly received, and I invited them to our Christmas services—not that services had been neglected, for Sunday after Sunday, Mr.

ALBANY, HUDSON'S BAY

Broughton, Chrissie's husband, had conducted an English service; while young Mr. Vincent, the archdeacon's son, conducted an Indian one.

'Christmas Day dawned bright and clear. Before it was light the church was nearly filled with Indians, many having come in from their distant hunting-grounds to join in the festival. The singing was hearty, and the attention throughout very deep. As I read and spoke of the love of Christ, the manger of Bethlehem, the joy of the angels, the adoration of the shepherds, and the blessings Christ is willing to dispense to all who believe on Him, we all, I think, felt that Christ was with us of a truth. At four o'clock another congregation assembled. There were only two or three persons present who had ever seen England, yet the English language is well spoken by nearly everyone, and this service was as enjoyable as its predecessor had been. In the afternoon we had our third service, in Indian, and after the sermon twenty-eight of us knelt around the Lord's table.

'On New Year's Day, at five o'clock, I was serenaded by the "Albany Band." It consists of a drum, a violin, and a triangle, and on these three instruments our New Year's morning music was discoursed. Two hours and a half later there was a good congregation in the church, in which we met to return thanks for the mercies of the past year, and to ask a continuance of them during that so lately begun. I preached on Psalm xc. 12, "So teach us to number our days, that we may apply our hearts unto wisdom." Directly after breakfast we began to prepare for visitors, the entire population of Albany. For their consumption a large quantity of currant wine, cakes, and tea was provided, together with an abundance of sweets, intended mostly for the little ones. About ten o'clock all the men-servants of the establishment came in, dressed in their best, and, after wishing us a "Happy New Year," all sat around the room, and a lively conversation began. But what a difference now from the old days! Then, nearly all were Europeans, for very few natives were fit for the service in any capacity; now, all are natives. Shop-master, blacksmith, cooper, carpenters, storekeeper—not one of them has ever seen more than five hundred people at one time, and now all would be able to take their places in the workshops of England, speaking and reading English as if born in England. The oldest present I married four-and-thirty years ago, and he and his wife have now a goodly number of grandchildren. All are very well conducted, nearly all are communicants. What would the state of things have been had there been no mission in the country!

'The men and lads having departed, after an interval the wives, daughters, and young children came in, and a goodly number they were, healthy and strong; while in colour they were of all shades, from pure white to dark brown. All spoke English well—quite as good, nay, very much better English than is spoken by many of the working-classes in England; while all above the age of seven years can read fairly. This was a very enjoyable party, the enjoyment culminating in a grand scramble for sweets.

'After our dinner the Indians all came in again. There was a little speech-making, and a great deal of cake-eating and tea-drinking; after which grandfather, and daughter, and son-in-law, and the four young grandsons, had the evening to themselves, and a very pleasant one they had.

'New Year's Day was over. A few days more passed, and then on the morning of January 5 the sledge and dogs—now thirteen—were once more on the ice. We started. The cold was terrible, thirty-five degrees below zero, and a strong wind blowing. Six hours afterwards we were in our tent, making a fire, over which a kettle of good coffee was soon boiling. The next day, and still the next day, the wind was equally strong, the temperature nearly as low, and the atmosphere filled with fine particles of snow. The third day was our last out, and at three o'clock in the afternoon I was once more in my old quarters. I found all well, and at once fell into the old routine of work.'

CHAPTER XVII

THE PACKET MONTH

'FEBRUARY is the most interesting month of the year to us; it is the "Packet Month," the month in which we have our one communication with the outer world during the dreary months of our long winter. On the third day of the month, 1886, we had two arrivals—Mr. Broughton and Mr. Vincent, the agents from Rupert's House and Albany—each bringing the "packet" of his respective district. The news was generally good, but from the smallest post of all—English River—came the saddest possible. Three children of the only resident there, the whole of whom were in robust health in the autumn, were cut off by diphtheria in the course of eleven days, in the beginning of winter.

'On the 5th, a little after breakfast, the "packeters" were espied crossing the river, in snow-shoes. Directly they arrived their precious load was transferred to the Hudson's Bay Company offices; there hammers and chisels, seized by willing hands, soon knocked the covers from the boxes, and the work of distribution commenced. All my letters are thrown

AN INDIAN TRAVELLING ON SNOW-SHOES

L

upon the table; the eye travels along them somewhat nervously, brightening as this and that well-known hand is seen, looking with sad inquiry at such as are black-edged, and disappointedly anxious if those expected most are not forthcoming. The receiving of letters is good; the answering of them, when they are many in number, is great drudgery. Telephones have not come our way yet, and the nearest telegraph office is about four hundred miles distant.

'On the 7th the break-up of our party commenced. Mr. Broughton started for Albany. In the evening the packet was closed, and the next morning the "packeters" once more turned their faces southwards, and set out on their three hundred miles' tramp to Abbitibbee; thence the packet will be forwarded to Temiscamingue and Matawa, and twelve days more will take it to England.'

In March Mr. Nevitt left Moose Fort for Rupert's House, with the purpose of at length establishing a permanent mission at that station. 'For many years I had longed, with a most earnest longing, to see a missionary established there, until the heart was beginning to grow sick, and at last I determined to give up all help here at Moose, rather than allow my dear hungering people to remain longer without a shepherd to watch over them. I therefore told Mr. Nevitt to prepare for departure. This was neither unexpected nor disagreeable to him. A train of dogs and a sledge arrived from Rupert's House, which, after a few days' stay here, were to return thither with supplies of various kinds. Here was an opportunity not to be neglected. A few necessaries were collected and placed in the sledge, and, after having been commended to God's providential care, he set out for his new home, accompanied by two members of his future flock. One of them, Richard Swanson, was educated at our mission school at Moose; the other, Samuel Wesley, at the school at Albany.'

This spring there was a flood of a somewhat serious character at Moose. At three o'clock one morning in April, a heavy crash awoke all the inhabitants of the fort. An immense field of ice was borne in on the land, the water rose several feet at once, and everyone was on the alert. Nothing serious happened during the day, and Mrs. Peck, who was staying at Moose on account of her health, and the servant retired to bed about half-past nine.

At eleven the alarm bell was rung; almost everyone fled to the factory; the bishop took Mrs. Peck to one of the mission buildings further from the river, he himself remaining up to watch. Early the next morning they went to the company's establishment, where the bishop spent the day in bed, for he had passed the greater part of two nights without removing his clothes. Had the water risen only a little higher, the results would have been very disastrous. As it was, the scene all around was desolate in the extreme. However, Easter Sunday dawned bright and fair, the ice yielded to the current, and the water found again its proper channel.

When May came that year the snow had disappeared, the grass was becoming green, the air was mild and genial, and the birds were singing in the woods, despite the huge ice blocks which still were lying there. June, 1886, was the finest month the bishop had ever known in Hudson's Bay. Generally at that time winter has scarcely departed, and the trees show no appearance of life ; but now the poplars were bursting into leaf, the willows were already clothed with the first fresh flush of green, birds hopped among the branches, the cattle bells told that the cows were grazing near at hand, and the meadows formed one superb carpet. The hearts of all in that sterile land rejoiced, but Moose was comparatively empty, for the season being so advanced the Indian brigades had left early.

'Before starting they came to me, mostly one by one, each to give me his little confidence. One said : "I have not yet given my subscription to the church, and will give it now, but I am not able to do as much as I did last year ; then I made a good fur hunt, this year but a very poor one ; but I know we must not appear before God empty, so I will do what I can." Another said : "Pray for me while I am away. I know I have given you a great deal of trouble, and I am very sad at heart at thinking how wickedly and foolishly I have acted, but I hope I shall be very different in future." Another : "My wife has been taken ill ; I shall be glad if you will go to her, and read and pray by her." Another and another and yet another required a book, some two, a Prayer and hymn-book ; then all descend to their boats, which speedily make from the shore, and, impelled by heavy oars, they commence their journey.'

On July 1, 1886, the bishop wrote: 'It is hot; we are being literally baked, and from the heat there is scarcely any shelter, for the houses, all made of wood, retain the heat in such a manner that they are like ovens. But we are getting exactly the weather we need, with a prospect of very fair crops of potatoes and turnips, and, what is better, of being free from the terrible epidemics which have caused so much sorrow during the last few years. The packet, or rather the first instalment of it, reached us late in the evening of Sunday, June 20—the first news from the outer world since the beginning of February; and then for a day or two we were deep in letters and newspapers. But the 23rd was the great day of arrivals, for we had no less than three. In the early morning, soon after getting up, we saw a large boat coming up the river; the boat from Rupert's House, coming for supplies for the mission. Presently we saw a large canoe, and from the shape of it we knew it must be from Fort George, and that our dear friend and earnest worker, Mr. Peck, must be in it; and very soon I had the pleasure of grasping by the hand a sunburnt, weather-beaten son of toil, who, after more than four months of hard and continuous work—of travel by snow-shoe, dog-sledge, and canoe—returned to his wife, to find her as well as she had ever been in her life, and hoping to see a steam-launch, which had been sent out for his use, ready for sea, that he might at once leave again for his northern home. But in this he was disappointed, for the job of putting the various parts together was more difficult than we had anticipated. During the whole month the hammers were giving forth their noise rom four o'clock in the morning until night. All the mission staff, setting aside their work, spent day after day in steaming planks, nailing them on, in sawing wood, in caulking, and painting, and puttying. On the same day came the remainder of the packet.

'Throughout the first days of July all were still occupied with Mr. Peck's boat. The hammering went on; nail after nail was driven, and the caulking went on incessantly; the air was filled with the odour of burning tar. On the 9th the craft was ready to be launched. In the evening almost everyone in the place was at the mission, either as a spectator or a helper. We had a long way to drag the boat, and this occupied nearly two hours. Then we had the pleasure of seeing it descend quietly into the water, in which, I trust, it will make many voyages for the extension of the kingdom of our Lord among the Indians and Eskimo of the wide district of East Main.

'All now were busy in preparation for departure, for the sooner our friends arrived at their place of destination the better. Saturday was so employed, and so was Monday; while on Sunday we held three delightful services, at two of which Mr. Peck preached.

'On Tuesday the boat was loaded with casks of flour, cans of beef and salt pork, chests of tea, and all the other etceteras needful to housekeeping, for at Fort George the nearest shop is three hundred miles away. About two o'clock in the afternoon it went down the river. An hour afterwards, Mr. and Mrs. Peck and our kind doctor entered a canoe and, amid the blessing and prayers of a large number of people assembled on the bank of the river, they set off. Canoe and boat went on to Ship's Sands, an island eight miles down the river. Here they passed the night. The next day Mr. Peck went on board his boat, while Mrs. Peck continued her voyage in the canoe. In a few days East Main was reached; here Mrs. Peck rested for a night. East Main was formerly the principal Hudson's Bay Company's station in James' Bay, but the river silting up and preventing the annual ship from getting near enough for protection from the open sea, Moose became the headquarters of the fur trade. A hundred and fifty miles had yet to be travelled, which would occupy five or six days. At last Fort George, a few miles up the Fort George River, was reached, the home of the faithful missionary and his brave and faithful wife.

'When the Pecks had left, an influenza cold attacked almost everyone at Moose, persistently clinging to the sufferers; but is it any wonder that we have colds here, when sometimes there is a difference of over fifty degrees between the temperature of the morning

THE CHURCH AT FORT GEORGE

and evening? In the morning we may be almost roasting: before evening the wind may have suddenly chopped round to the north, and, sweeping over the frozen bay, may render fires and warm coats desirable, if not necessary.'

CHAPTER XVIII

CHURCHILL AND MATAWAKUMMA

IN 1886 the bishop wrote with much thankfulness of the location of the Rev. J. Lofthouse at Churchill—'the last house in the world,' as he called it, for there is no other between it and the North Pole. Churchill boasts, however, of quite a little colony of English and half-caste Chipwyans, Eskimo, and Crees. The Chipwyans are difficult to trade with, and apt to avoid a station for years if their demands are not complied with. They are cruel to their wives and their dogs, and are terrible thieves, but they stand in great fear of the Eskimo. The Eskimo of Churchill are not so bloodthirsty as their brethren in the west, who come in with their faces marked with red ochre, to indicate that they have committed a murder during the winter, a mark in which they glory, for in their opinion there is more honour in killing a human being than in killing a walrus or white bear.

Out of the world as it seems, Churchill is a busy place with the coming and going of Crees, Eskimo, and Chipwyans. The annual ship goes thither from York Factory, and boats have to be built for the loading and unloading of the cargo, as well as

CHURCHILL IN SUMMER

or carrying on the trade further north with Mable Island. Food is very dear, and is obtained with toil and difficulty. In summer, porpoises are hunted; in winter, bears, wolves, and foxes are shot. The cold is intense, and quantities of wood must be hewn, and haüled home on sledges drawn by the Eskimo dog. The short summer will scarcely allow any garden produce to come to perfection. A few very poor and puny potatoes are grown, which are highly prized by the Europeans, and carefully eked out. A very little hay is made for the winter fodder of the cows; which, however, gladly eat the nourishing white moss, which is the food of the reindeer.

'I must tell you,' says the bishop, with a spice of humour, 'about the Churchill cows, for they are—or were—a curious lot. There were three of them. About one there was nothing very particular, except that it was somewhat of a dwarf. The second went about harnessed, for, Churchill pasture not making her particularly fat, she was so supple that she required no milkmaid to milk her; she did it herself, and seemed to enjoy the exercise. The harness supported a bag, which enclosed the udder, and which prevented her from indulging in a draught of new milk. The third had an artificial tail. The poor brute had been off at a little distance from the place, when she was set upon by some wolves; she bellowed, and at once made for home, where she arrived almost frightened to death, and without a tail. What was to be done now? The flies were in myriads, and, if she had no protection against them, they would put her to a much more cruel death than that threatened by the wolves. A happy thought struck one of the colony of fifty. They had a dead cow's tail lying in the store! Why not use that? The suggestion was at once acted upon; the tail was attached to the stump by means of some twine, and over it was tied some canvas, well saturated with Stockholm tar. It was a great success, and the creature was again able to do battle with her diminutive but persevering foes.'

In undertaking the distant station of Churchill, in the midst of a dreary waste, Mr. Lofthouse had a life of self-denial before him, as well as very serious work, not the least of which was the necessity for learning three languages, neither of them bearing any resemblance to the other. For example, the phrase 'It is good' is in Chipwyan *nazo*, in Cree *milwashiu*, and in Eskimo *peyokumme*.

Far away from Moose, five hundred miles distant, very difficult to reach—the journey to it occupying about twenty days—is the station of Matawakumma. Long and dangerous rapids have to be ascended, long and disagreeable portages to be crossed, one of which is four miles in length. One long lake—Kinokummisse, meaning 'long lake'—must be traversed, and another—Matawakumma, 'The meeting of the waters'—must be gone over.

The station is very prettily situated on a long point of land which runs almost across the lake. There are a few houses representing the fur-trading establishment. At a short distance is the modest parsonage-house and neat church, both of which have been almost

ON THE CHURCHILL RIVER

entirely erected by the Rev. J. Saunders' own hands. It was the most isolated station in Moosonee, but it is so no longer, as at only two days' journey distant runs the great Canadian Pacific railroad, by which all supplies are now introduced into that part of the country.

There is at present no danger of starvation here, but formerly, when all supplies were got up from Moose, and were consequently limited, great privation was frequently experienced. If the rabbits failed, famine stared the inhabitants in the face. The worst year ever known was the one the bishop first spent in the country, when a fourth of the entire population died, some from actual starvation, the rest being killed and eaten by their friends! The tales of that terrible winter are heartrending in the extreme. The most painful case was that of a man and his wife who lost their whole family of six children.

Among the Indians of Matawakumma was one named Arthur Martin.

'I forget his Indian name,' says the bishop. 'I give the name he received at his baptism. At the time referred to he was a young man, and was not subjected to as great privations as some of his countrymen. I received him into the Church in 1852, and in 1854 I received his wife, on my first visit to Matawakumma, where I married them. Many of the Indians there clung very closely to their old superstitions, and the drum and the conjuring tents were in constant requisition. Some of them still hold back, not having yet taken the Saviour to their hearts.

'But this was not the case with Arthur and his wife; when once they had put their hand to the plough, they looked not back again. Their Saviour was their all in all. They both learnt to read, and made themselves well acquainted with the books as they came out in the Ojibbeway language, the only one they knew, and they did their best to train their children in the ways of the Lord. Their eldest son, Louis, one of the most intelligent Indians I have ever known, followed in his father's steps, and eventually became a valuable catechist in the mission. His letters were excellent, while to Mr. Saunders he was invaluable, assisting him in everything; for he handled hammer, axe, and paddle with equal facility, and he was his constant companion in his journeys through the country. I had hopes that eventually I might ordain him, and thus increase both his influence and usefulness among his countrymen; but this was not to be. He went with Mr. Saunders to their railway station, Biscotasing; in getting into a carriage while in motion, he fell and injured his leg. It required amputation; the operation was performed, and it was hoped that all would go well; but a few days after mortification set in, and the end soon came. He seemed necessary for our work; it never occurred to us that we might be obliged to do without him. Truly

God moves in a mysterious way.

'The death of this son was a heavy blow to his father, now growing old; but he was soon resigned to the will of God, and went on his Christian course. Like Job of old, he was tried by personal suffering; in that, too, his faith remained firm and steadfast. A mist and darkness came over him—blindness took possession of both his eyes. It was thought that his sight might be restored by an operation, and he was sent down to Moose for that purpose. He was quite alone, having no relative with him, but he was taken good care of by a Christian woman, who tended him with sisterly devotion.

'For awhile he kept well, was never absent from the house of God; then weakness attacked him in the legs, and he could no longer attend the services, yet not a word of complaint fell from him. He longed for news from home, and this he received; his wife was very unwell, but hoped soon to see him back with her again. Inflammation of the lungs set in, and in three or four days he had passed away. God was with him in his trial, and supported him. He made all his bed in his sickness. I saw him on the day of his death, September 12, between the morning and afternoon services. Blind and speechless, he lay in his tent surrounded by a few Christian friends, who said that he was quite insensible. He regained consciousness as I spoke to him of Jesus and His love. When I asked him whether he felt Jesus near, a joyous, assuring smile came over his countenance, more expressive than the most eloquent of speeches.

'He was waiting in peace the Master's call, and it was not long in coming. I commended him to God in prayer, and, shaking him warmly by the hand hurried off to church to conduct service. Soon afterwards the messenger arrived to summon him to the Master's presence. With the Lord he went through the dark valley; with Him he crossed the dividing river, and then entered the joy of his Lord.'

CHAPTER XIX

A DAY AT BISHOP'S COURT

THE bishop was now contemplating a visit to England. He had not seen his wife or children for six years, and looked forward to meeting them in the fatherland once more. He hoped to leave Moose in June 1888, to be in time for the Lambeth Conference in July. He intended the summer following to visit York and Churchill, in North Moosonee, which could be more conveniently done in starting from England. 'To visit them from Moose,' he said, 'would involve a very, very long and expensive journey, and a winter's stay, which is now quite unnecessary, seeing that both stations are well occupied, and I can do much more for the missions in England than I could there.'

In February 'the packet' came, and friends from all the surrounding stations gathered together to bring and receive letters, and to wish him God speed on his proposed journey.

May-day came, and a depth of snow lay upon the ground. The river was still ice-bound. All Nature was hushed, not even the 'goose call' was heard, for the weather was so severe that the geese kept close. One of the mission party went off early, and sat for many hours in his goose-stand with his decoy geese professionally arranged, but he returned unsuccessful.

The bishop too was up early. 'I always am,' he wrote, 'wishing to have an hour of perfect quiet before the duties of the day begin. I generally read a chapter of the Hebrew Bible every morning. I was never taught to read it. I never heard a word of it read, except what is contained in the English Bible; yet I have read the Hebrew Bible right through, carefully and grammatically. Hebrew is a very difficult language, but it is not insurmountable, and the word impossible must never find its way into the vocabulary of one who intends to devote himself to mission work. A man who is daunted by difficulties, who thinks there is a possibility of his not acquiring the language of the people to whom he may be sent, had far better never put his foot on ship-board for foreign work. He will in the end prove a bitter disappointment, both to himself and those who are associated with him. "I can do all things through Christ, who strengtheneth me," must be the watchword of every one who enters the diocese of Moosonee. And now look at the 84th Psalm in the Revised Version; observe the beauty of the sixth verse. It is superlatively sweet and consolatory: "Passing through the valley of weeping, they make it a place of springs; yea, the early rain covereth it with blessings." Then I read the third chapter of St. Paul's Epistle to the Ephesians, in Greek; what beauty, too, there is in this chapter, especially in verses fourteen to nineteen.

'Before I had completed the second chapter my

three young grandsons, Fred, Arthur, and Sydney Broughton, had come into my sitting-room to wish me good-morning, when the two elder ones remained to receive a lesson from me, which they do every day. Family prayers were held at eight o'clock punctually, for I am a very punctual man, never keeping anyone waiting, and we then discussed our frugal breakfast. There was myself and my daughter Chrissie—her husband having some time before gone to the Hudson's Bay Company's establishment to preside at breakfast there; my two grandsons, and the Rev. E. Richards, my much beloved native helper; Arthur and his beautiful little mischievous sister, Gertrude, taking their breakfast with their nurse in another room. We had one rabbit, the last, I am afraid, for the season, a little imported bacon, and some good bread to eat, while to drink we had excellent coffee.

'A little after ten o'clock I should have had the first class of our school in my room, but thinking the shooting of a goose or duck as necessary an accomplishment in Moosonee as writing a letter, I had given the bigger boys a week's holiday to go goose-hunting, and had moreover promised a prize to the most successful hunter. Then our doctor came in, and we discussed the various cases under his care. I take a deep interest in his work, and always assist him when he requires help. I am extremely sorry to find that the condition of a good young man, married, with one child, is very critical. Consumption will, I fear, at no distant day make him its victim. For dinner we had a little cold beef, a part of the store laid by last autumn, when the whole beef of the year was killed; it was still quite fresh and good; some mashed potatoes, and afterwards a nice raspberry tart. We drink spruce beer at dinner, a most wholesome non-intoxicating drink, refreshing and an excellent digestive. After dinner much of my time was spent with two of my sick folk, who delight in hearing the Word of God read to them.'

The rest of the bishop's day was filled up with study with his divinity students, the ever continuing work of translation, and lessons to an evening class of young men of the Hudson's Bay Company. He never permitted himself an idle moment. 'He had,' he said, 'no desire to rust out.' And there seemed little danger of it.

On May 31, 1888, the bishop left Moose Fort for England. It was his fourth visit in the course of thirty-seven years of missionary life in the Great Lone Land.

'What a day,' he writes, 'was my last Sunday at Moose! How fully were all the services attended! What a large number of communicants, and how solemn was our ordination service, when the Rev. E. Richards was made priest! How painful were the partings of the succeeding week, for every one at Moose is to me as a son or a daughter. As the hour of departure approached a crowd assembled at the head of the island, where I was to embark. At four o'clock I stepped into my canoe, and standing up, the people being on the high bank, I gave them my fatherly blessing. I had two companions to go with me to Canada—a young grandson, eight years of age, and a most loved young friend, who was to stay with her uncle in Montreal. My daughter and her children accompanied me, to remain for the night, and the evening was one of cheerful sadness. Our encampment seemed like a small canvas village, so many had come off in their canoes. After the tents were all erected, we soon had a good fire roaring in the forest, by which we cooked our meal; then we had a very solemn service, and by half-past nine the fires were out, the tents were closed, and all was quiet.

'We were astir in the early morning, when we again bent the knee together in prayer, after which the last farewells were uttered, the last kiss given—my last to my sweet little granddaughter, Gertrude, who was too young to understand the nature of "Good-bye," and who would for many a day wonder why grandpapa did not come and have a romp with her, and take his accustomed place at table. Then we descended to our respective canoes; they to return to Moose, we to pursue our solitary way up the mighty river, until we came to the great sign of modern civilisation, the iron road of the steam-engine at Missenabie, a station of the Canadian Pacific Railway. I had five Indians with me, all good fellows, Christians, in whom I had the fullest confidence, and who, I knew, would do their very best to bring us in safety to the place of our destination. They divided themselves into two bodies, and took turn and turn about at the tracking. A long line was attached to the canoe; to this one party harnessed itself, for in going against the stream the paddle is but little used, the principal work being done by the tracking line and pole—the latter a powerful instrument of propulsion about nine feet long, and shod with iron, wonderfully useful among the rapids.

'At breakfast time we all went ashore; a fire was kindled, the kettle boiled, a little meat cooked, and, sitting on boxes or stones, the meal was consumed; after which we continued our way until dinner-time, when there was another halt. Then we went on again until eight o'clock, when we put up for the night. This was quite a business, for we could not encamp everywhere. We went up into the woods; axes were brought into requisition, and a large space was cleared; the marquees were put up, and everything was made as comfortable as possible, so that presently we were quite at home; supper, conversation, and service finished the day, when we lay down, grateful for continued mercies.

'In the morning, during the breakfast hour, all met near the fire; we first had a hymn, after which I read a portion of Scripture, and prayers from the Prayer Book. Prayer-time was to us a season of great refreshment. We had sometimes heavy rains; this caused us much trouble, greatly increasing the difficulty and danger of the rapids. Frequently we were all obliged to get ashore, and make our way as best we could through the pathless woods, where the fallen trees were lying about in every direction. This was intensely hard work.

'On one occasion we had ascended a terrible and

A LARGE CANOE SHOOTING A RAPID

long rapid, and had got by the easiest side of the stream just opposite the foot of our longest portage, but between us and it ran the swollen and fiercely flowing river. We all grasped a paddle firmly, and bending with our full strength dashed out into the stream; we could get no further, and were swept down like lightning into the boiling rapid. The sight was the most dangerous I had ever witnessed, but the men were equal to the emergency. Turning round in the canoe, the bow became the stern, and we were kept clear of the rocks which threatened our destruction.

'Then on we went again to face fresh dangers, to meet with new difficulties; still ever onwards, till on Saturday morning we came into the smooth waters of the Missenabie Lake. Missenabie was a small and inconsiderable post which up to this time had been buried deep in the wilderness, but which by the carrying of the Canadian Pacific Railway through the country, had been brought to the very confines of the civilised world, being only fifty miles from a railway station.'

After spending Sunday at Missenabie, a day's journey brought the travellers to Missenabie station. The Indians heard for the first time the voice of the 'steam giant.' Paddling with some difficulty under the wooden bridge which is the path of the 'fire-sledge,' the station was presently reached. It was a dreary spot—a tent or two, a couple of tumble-down stores, a house or two for the railway officials, and multitudes of mosquitoes. A railway truck was the bishop's parlour ; in the booking-office he held services in three languages, Cree, Ojibbeway, and English. Very early in the morning the train came in from the West, and carried the party away. To the little grandson, aged eight, all things were new and strange. A lad passed through the cars with oranges and apples for sale ; the child had never seen either an apple or an orange in his life, and when one of each was handed to him, he asked, 'Grandpapa, which is which ?'

At Ottawa, Montreal, and the grand old town of Quebec, our travellers had some few days' rest. At the latter place, Master Fred saw a Punch and Judy show for the first time, and enjoyed it ; and the bishop enjoyed it 'almost as much as he.' Grandfather and grandson visited the site of the battle which gave Quebec to England, and the monuments erected to the memory of the brave Generals Montcalm and Wolfe. Twelve days later they were in England. 'But,' says the bishop, 'the heart was still far away across the water, amid the secluded forests of Moosonec.'

CHAPTER XX

CLOSING LABOURS

BISHOP HORDEN did not spend a very great many months in England. He left again on May 22, 1889, the parting from wife and family being softened by the hope of shortly returning to them. Taking steamer direct for Quebec, he went on from thence to Montreal—'one of the most beautifully situated cities in the world, containing fine shops, a noble quay, many grand houses, and a large number of very fine churches.'

The following evening he took his place in the train going west, to spend three days and two nights in it. The car was crowded, and each day he—indefatigable man that he was—gave a much appreciated lecture to the occupants packed closely together around him. After passing through hundreds of miles of wilderness he at last landed at Winnipeg, the capital of the West. Two or three hours later he was sitting in the Parliament House, witnessing the conferring of university degrees by the Metropolitan, amongst the students being Miss Holmes, the first lady who had taken a degree in Manitoba. On Sunday there was an ordination and confirmation, and in the evening Bishop Horden preached in the cathedral, although he was suffering from a severe cold contracted during his long railway journey. The following day he started by rail and steamer for Norway House, which he reached on June 14.

There used to be stirring times at Norway House. Here the great council was held. Here in olden time the Governor of the Hudson's Bay Company, who possessed more real power than the most arbitrary of sovereigns, held his court annually, and to it flocked the principal officers of the company. The affairs of the country were discussed, and everything was arranged for another year. During the whole summer the greatest activity prevailed. Boats were continually arriving and departing; now an immense brigade from York Factory, then another from the Saskatchewan or the Mackenzie River district. The dwelling-houses were crowded, and the great stores were constantly receiving or giving out supplies.

But the railway and steamers have changed all this, and among other results have brought about the downfall of Norway House. Goods for the interior are no longer sent to York Factory, and thence by boat to the various stations. They are forwarded to the Saskatchewan by rail and steamer, and thence onward to the interior. Now Norway House supplies only two or three trading posts in its immediate district. Very few officers and few men are required for the business. The stores lie empty, and the great square is almost deserted.

Bishop Horden spent two Sundays here, waiting for the boats to Oxford House, whence he journeyed on to York Factory. Then he set off for Churchill, another journey of two hundred miles.

A peaceful voyage of nine days in a schooner, the first that for twenty years had visited York Factory, brought the bishop to Moose Fort. It was quite dark when he landed, but a great crowd had gathered on the beach to welcome him, chief amongst them his daughter, Mrs. Broughton, and her husband, and their three youngest children, and Archdeacon Vincent, who had been in charge at Bishop's Court.

'I was really at home, and felt so overjoyed and so thankful; I was happy, and so seemed all around me. Monday was devoted to the affairs of the mission, and it gratified me to find that things had gone on so well during my absence. I visited all the people in their houses, for they are very dear to me, and found all well.'

But his own house was lonely, and would be lonelier still in the winter, for the Broughtons were to be now stationed at Rupert's House. He had not been expected to return so soon to Moose; the archdeacon had the work there well in hand, whilst at Albany Mr. and Mrs. Nevitt were fully installed. He himself needed some little quiet and rest. He decided, therefore, to go with his daughter and grandchildren to Rupert's House for the next months.

The Moose ship, Lady Head, had already arrived. The season was advanced, a parting service was held, and once more the bishop went on board the Mink, and sailed with his dear ones for Rupert's House. Here he came in contact with Indians from various stations, bringing in furs for barter at the factory. The Rev. E. Richards assisted him in all his ministrations. A cheerful Christmas was followed by quiet work, and then a busy and a happy Eastertide, notwithstanding the 'snow which lay several feet deep on the ground, biting winds, and the death-like appearance of all Nature.'

The spring was very dreary. There was nothing for the geese to feed upon, and the hunters came home evening after evening having shot nothing. When the Indians from the surrounding districts came in, there was amongst them one very sad and reduced party. Where were the rest? All, to the number of eighteen, had perished from starvation.

As the summer approached, the bishop went northward to East Main River—now a small outpost, but once the most important place in the bay. About one hundred Indians had met together there, and every moment was made the most of, for they seldom saw a clergyman.

The bishop thence went in a boat to Fort George. This is almost the most interesting bit of travel in the country. High and rocky islands, some of them well wooded, others majestically rugged, rise in constant succession.

A week was spent at the Fort, and then, with Mr. Peck as his companion, the bishop pushed on to the dreary storm-beaten land of Great Whale River —a hard and difficult journey along an inhospitable and dangerous coast. Sometimes they met a few Indians on the way, and the desert was made to rejoice with 'some of the songs of Zion.'

One morning they put ashore among a body of Eskimo, who had their books with them. The bishop heard them all read; for one woman, who could not read as well as the rest, they made the apology that she had but just recently joined them from the north, and could not be expected to do very well yet; but she was getting on, for they taught her every day. The next day, and half of the following, was spent here, then the travellers proceeded, the canoe flying before a threatened storm. Just before midnight they reached the mouth of the river, and two or three hours afterwards the storm broke with terrible violence, lasting without intermission for a couple of days.

'Three days of intense work (I wish it could have been three weeks), and the schooner was ready for sea; so, leaving Mr. Peck to continue his labours, I took a passage kindly granted me, and bidding farewell to all, I set off on my way south.'

The bishop was much gratified with the progress made by the Eskimo, their earnestness was so evident, their attention so fixed; his heart was lifted in gratitude to God. After another week spent at Fort George, his mission completed, his face was once more turned homewards, and he reached Moose just about ship time. 'In all this journey God's hand has been on me for good.'

Soon after the bishop had returned to Moose, Mr.

and Mrs. Nevitt went to take charge of Rupert's House, the Rev. E. Richards and his wife coming to assist the bishop at Moose. Great preparations were made for the Christmas of 1890. The old mission ox brought home several loads of pine and cedar-brush from the woods for the church decorations. On Christmas Eve a high tea was provided at Bishop's Court for the joyous band of workers, a dish of splendid trout gracing the hospitable board. Christmas morning dawned not too cold for enjoyment, and hearty, cheery services followed throughout the day. A feast had been planned for the school-children. Cakes were made by 'the Rev. E. Richards and his wife;' a large heap of biscuits were provided from the bishop's own store; huge kettles were suspended in the school-yard; tea, sugar, and milk were there in abundance, and one afternoon in the Christmas week the scholars all assembled and enjoyed a substantial meal.

A Christmas-tree followed, which Mr. and Mrs. Richards had decorated with artificial flowers and ornaments, lights and gifts. The children's parents were there, and the European residents and all stood round the tree, and sang 'God save the Queen.'

> Muncto pinache Kicheake-maskwas,
> O Pimache; Melche puskilakat,
> Kitche milwaletuk Kinwaish
> Pimatesit, O Pimache.

Other gatherings there were that joyous Christmastide spent by the bishop amongst his own especial flock; and doubtless, as he said, for many days to come the pleasures and wonders of those happy evenings were subjects of comment in every house.

The bishop had brought with him from York Factory a very promising youth, Isaiah Squirrel by name, whom he hoped to train under his own eye for the Christian ministry. He was now at Moose, 'learning all sorts of things, and showing himself very teachable.'

At the beginning of the year 1891 the bishop announced with thankful joy, 'I have now ready for the press the Pentateuch, Isaiah, Jeremiah, the Lamentations, Ezekiel, and Daniel; the Psalms and New Testament have been in print some years. The whole Bible will, I trust, form the crown of my missionary life. I take the deepest delight in this translation work, which has always engaged very much of my time and attention.'

May was cold and damp this year; snow and ice abounded, and the ground was still almost bare of pasture. Flocks of snowbirds were about, which were pursued by the boys with bows and arrows, and a few American robins sang among the leafless trees; but the geese, like everything else, failed. Day after day the Indian went forth to his goose-stand in the marsh, arranged his decoys, loaded his guns, and sat and called, hoping that a flight of geese would be enticed by the friendly voice to come and visit his flock of dummies. But no geese came, and the hunter returned each evening disconsolate and supperless to his tent. When the kettle on the fire is well filled with *mechim* (food), there is joy in the camp, and the Indian does not heed the weather—storm rain, and snow are to him of no account; but with wife and children hungering around him things are sad indeed; and thus they were in the month of May.

The summer proved a sickly one in all the district. In June the bishop went to Rupert's House, and whilst working there from morning till night amongst the great body of Indians congregated for the season, the influenza broke out, and he became at once doctor and nurse, until he was himself attacked. He was for some time very unwell, and his voice went. Mr. and Mrs. Nevitt had left to go home by the annual ship, Mr. Nevitt's health having failed, and Mr. Richards was at Moose, so he could not, and would not, give in, except for a day or two. Happily, he was in the house of his dear daughter Chrissie, where every possible attention was given him. 'The voice returned, but strength was slow in coming.' Then his much loved little granddaughter was attacked very severely, and it was a sore trial to have to leave her, still hovering between life and death, when he was obliged to return to Moose. A long time elapsed before he could hear from Rupert's House. Then at last came a little letter from the child herself to tell of her recovery.

In August, 1891, an event happened which was destined to be of very great importance to the diocese of Moosonee. This was the arrival at Fort Moose of the Rev. J. A. Newnham. The bishop had met and conversed with Mr. Newnham on his visit to Montreal in the previous year, and finding how his heart was yearning for the mission cause in Moosonee, he had invited him to join him there.

'I was charmed,' wrote Mr. Newnham, 'with my first acquaintance with Moose. My room in the bishop's house looks over a small encampment of about forty tents and sixty dogs. Just now is the busy season; the hay is being carried, and the ship unloaded, but quite a congregation gathers every evening at 6·30 for a short service. I attended it my first evening on shore, and was much struck with the hearty responses, and the clear and true singing of our well-known hymn tunes.'

After the service Mr. Newnham was introduced to the Indians, who greeted him with 'What cheer?' their form of 'How do you do?' As he sat in his study later, he could see them constantly coming to the house. The bishop never locked his door; even in the night it was left unfastened, and anyone might come to him at any hour for assistance or advice.

The bishop spent nearly the whole of this year at Moose, devoting all his leisure to the translation of the Cree Bible. He hoped to have the whole of the Old Testament ready for the press by mid-summer 1892. The revision of the New Testament, which had been printed many years before, would occupy him, he said, during the following winter. Again he wrote, 'and this will be the crowning work of my life, which will give spiritual food to my people for generations after my decease.' In less than a year after these words were penned, the earnest worker and writer lay in his grave, his work on earth done.

Towards the close of the year 1891, Archdeacon Vincent lost his wife, who had long been in a declining state. He brought her to Moose for burial. On December 20 the bishop preached the funeral sermon from the words, 'It is well.' These had been almost her last words before her death. Returning with the archdeacon to Albany, Bishop Horden there spent Christmas and New Year's Day. It was his last winter trip to Albany. 'The last,' he wrote, 'that I shall in all probability ever undertake. My first winter trip to Albany took place long, long ago, forty years ago this very month! I was then young and active, and thought nothing a hardship; I could sleep in the open, bivouac with the cold bright sky overhead, with the thermometer 40° below zero. I had no back, nor legs, nor shoulders; at least I had them as well as now, and much better; I merely did not know of their existence from any pain or inconvenience they caused me. But forty years make a difference. I know now that I have several members of my body, and these tell me in the most unmistakable manner that there must be no more getting over the rough snow and ice, and that the discomforts of a cold smoky tent must be no longer endured, unless there be absolute necessity. They tell me that, for the future, winter travelling must not be indulged in. And we must bow to the inevitable ; we cannot be always young ; the halting step and the grey head will come, and why should we dread their approach, when we know that " if the earthly house of our tabernacle be dissolved, we have a building from God, a house not made with hands, eternal in the heavens "?

'I am not, however, writing a sermon. I was about to speak of my last winter journey to Albany. I wished to go there, because there was very little hope of my going next summer. At seven o'clock on the morning of December 21, I was sitting in my sledge, and ten beautiful dogs in excellent condition were being harnessed thereto, each having its own single trace, by which it was attached to the sledge. The archdeacon occupied a second sledge. When all were harnessed, there was a great howling, and jumping, and tugging, for the dogs were anxious to be off, but the sledge was too firmly moored for their united strength until all was ready ; then the binding rope was cast off, howling ceased in a moment, each dog hauled with all his might, and we were away at the rate of ten miles an hour. The fine tails of the dogs were curled up over their backs, they were overjoyed to be once more on the road. The great pace was not long kept up, but settled into between five and six miles an hour, and so it continued throughout the day. To the music of our dog-bells we rushed down the river, soon losing sight of Moose, on past Middleborough Island, through Hay Creek, and then over a rough uncomfortable sort of plain at North Bluff, where stands the great beacon erected to attract the attention of our annual ship, and to tell her that she is nearing the place of her destination.

'Near the beacon we brought up for awhile, to give the dogs a rest. We had accomplished half of our day's work, and had come about eighteen miles. We are soon off again ; the air is very comfortable, and all our sensations are pleasurable as we run across North Bay, past Jarvis Bluff and Little Piskwamisk on to Piskwamisk, where our first "hotel" is situated—a small circular erection, gradually getting smaller towards the top, where a number of poles meet together; the whole is covered with snow, the doorway is blocked up with snow—as comfortless looking a place as can well be imagined. This is our hotel, and we at once set about making it as habitable as we can. The snow is dug away from the entrance with our snow-shoes, as well as from the sides, that there may be no dripping from its melting as the evening advances. Wood is carried in and a fire lit, and when a good beaf-steak has been fried and a strong cup of tea made and partaken of, we almost fall in love with our smoky hotel, and at any rate think it far preferable to the open bivouac in the heaven-covered forest.

'On the second day the weather was very warm, and much rain fell in the early part, but we continued on our way, having but twenty-five miles to travel, which brought us to our second hotel at Keshepinakok.

'On the third day we had forty miles of travel. The weather was colder and our dogs trotted on without much fatigue. About four o'clock in the afternoon we saw the settlement in the distance, and then the dogs, knowing that they were nearly home, put on extra speed, and we were soon in front of the factory. A steep bank had to be ascended, but there was no difficulty, for a number of men and boys ran down and gave their ready help, and I was soon in the middle of a large yard, receiving the warm welcome of all who had congregated there. One day at Albany, and then came Christmas Day, when I preached two sermons, one in English, the other in Indian; afterwards I had the examination of the candidates for confirmation belonging to the two congregations, Indian and English, with whom I was very well pleased; and the examination of the scholars in the school, who quite satisfied me, and I visited all the families in their respective houses. I also gave a feast to the Indians and another to the school children, and inspected some beautiful fox-skins. Quite a number of the silver fox came in during my visit. They are black, but the tips are white. They are too heavy for English wear, but are exported mostly to China. The late King George the Fourth had new coronation robes made for him, which were lined with the choicest parts of the silver fox skins, and for each skin forty guineas were paid; rather expensive robes, I should think.

'I found time to correct the proofs of two of my Indian books, which are printing in England. The days were well filled up and fled swiftly, and it seemed but a short time before I was compelled to say good-bye to Albany, and on the third day after we once more ran up Moose River, and received the congratulations of all my people, who had lined the banks to see me as I passed.'

The end of February, 1892, came before the 'packet' of that year arrived. All hope of its coming had died away, and many who had travelled hundreds of miles to meet it had been forced to travel back again without getting a letter to tell of those far away, or even a paper. 'Cruel, cruel!' said the sympathising bishop, and yet he was sometimes inclined to feel grateful for the very absence of news himself. 'Our outer door is opened,' he wrote, 'but twice or three times a year, and then we have a deluge of papers and a great number of letters, and we find the deluge almost as bad as the previous dearth.'

Moose was enjoying a mild winter, and food was plentiful, rabbits never more abundant, of pheasants there was no scarcity, and there was no sickness; the Moose doctor was enjoying quite a sinecure. Far otherwise was it with Rupert's House. The weather there also had been very mild, but rain had fallen in torrents, and the swamps around were giving forth miasma, which brought disease and death to the little settlement. Influenza and dysentery attacked almost every individual.

When the Rupert's House dogs brought the budget for the 'packet,' the bishop's share of news was a sad and gloomy one. Mr. Broughton wrote that the Indians were dying out from disease, and his own little daughter had again been attacked with influenza. Saddest tidings of all, four children had been frozen to death, almost close to the station. The father of those children was Weyawastum; he had died, as did also his wife, some years ago. The grandmother and her husband took the children under their care, she being a kind old body, and speaking very good English. They were spending the winter at Pontax Creek, about seven miles distant from the station, coming in occasionally for provisions, which were never denied them. At New Year the husband, named Huskey, came in to spend a few days at the place, and was there attacked by the prevailing disease, so severely as to be unable to return home. His wife and the children remained at Pontax Creek, no one feeling the least anxiety about them. They had a good tent and a sufficiency of provisions, and should those be consumed more would be given them. But one morning, someone walking down the river during a terribly cold spell of weather came upon a child lying dead, and hard frozen, only a mile from the establishment. And still farther on lay another, and yet another, and still another was found in the same condition. The tent was entered, but it was cold and silent, and there lay the dead body of kind old Betsy, the faithful grandmother. All were taken to Rupert's House, and buried in one grave. It must have been a terribly solemn event in that little settlement—five coffins entering the church in procession, four young lives passing away in such a manner. The full particulars will never be known, but it is supposed that while the grandmother was with the children in the tent she was suddenly taken ill, or being ill had become delirious, and the children being afraid, or wishing to obtain help for the old woman, had set off to get to the settlement, but the cold was too severe for them, and so all had perished.

If the winter at Moose had been late in coming, and mild when it came, it lasted long into the year 1892. On May 6 the bishop wrote:—

'Day succeeds day, and there is the same cold biting air, the same dark leaden sky and heavy snow-flakes, which have lately again and again thrown us back into apparent midwinter. I should be glad to write more cheerfully, but I must write what I see and know, and not give a picture from the imagination; what I write must be truth, and not romance. You can't conceive how anxiously we are longing for spring; to see our noble river rushing by, carrying on its bosom the laden boat, the beautiful canoe, the majestic vessel. But it is still blocked up, heavily fettered with its icy chains. The surface is still white, and an oppressive silence hangs over it; the fluttering haze has not yet appeared into which the mighty magician of long ago changed himself, appearing yearly in the spring, just before the breaking-up of the river, that he may meet his beautiful sister, the lovely American robin. She has already come, and it was with joy which can be felt, but not described, that I heard her singing her sweet song this morning, as if she would thus hasten the steps of her loitering brother, and bring him to cheer both her own heart and the hearts of all others who are anxiously awaiting his arrival. Whilst you enjoy sweet May weather, feel deeply thankful for it, and think of those in this wild lone land who are fighting the great Christian battle as your substitutes; pray for them, that their spirits droop not on account of the hardness of their surroundings, and show your sympathy practically by making greater and yet greater exertions in supporting the missionary cause.

'Now, looking out of my window, what can I see? Besides the cathedral and adjacent houses, I see the frozen surface of the river, dotted here and there with goose-stands, for this is the time for geese, and each goose-stand should be supplied with one or two smart hunters, whose decoy geese and their perfect imitation of the goose's call generally succeed in alluring the silly birds to their destruction. But the stands are unoccupied, the decoy geese are lying in heaps, the weather is so unpropitious that no birds are flying. They are delaying their journey to the sea coast, and are feeding in the plains in the interior; and when they come they will make but a short stay, and hurry forward to where they lay their eggs and bring up their families.

'But something exquisitely beautiful seems to enjoy the dreary waste—flocks of the snow bunting are constantly flitting by, alighting on the garden, the plain, and the dust heaps. When they first came they were white, but now they have begun to assume their summer garb, and clothe themselves in russet brown. They are not allowed to feed in peace. The fierce hawk hovers about, and occasionally swoops down and makes a capture; big boys and men are out with their guns, small boys are out with their bows and arrows, girls are out with their bird nets—all intent on business, for food is scarce, and those pretty birds are plump and fat, and said to be very good eating. And this is really all I can see from my window, except the dark distant pines, which fill up but do not enliven the landscape.

'You must not think that because I have such surroundings I am therefore dull and melancholy; such is by no means the case. God has blessed me with a sanguine temperament, and a great capacity for love of work, and this being the case, hope for better days and their speedy appearance causes me to look, in dark days, more to the future than the present; it gives no time for repining, or, as the people here say, thinking long.

'Well, thank God! I have written the last word of my Cree translation of the Bible. I had hoped to get it done by the time the river broke up, that I might then put my work aside for another winter, and devote myself to the Indians who will be coming in from the far interior; that I might take my long journeys to those distant centres of the mission whence the Indians cannot come; that Cree and Ojibbeway and Eskimo might again hear from my lips of the wondrous love of God in the gift to the world of His well-beloved Son; and my hope has been realised. The last word of the New Testament was written many years ago, but all will probably be re-written; all will at any rate be revised, if God permit, next winter, so as to bring it into accord with the Revised Version. It is, I think, a very good translation of the Authorised Version, and I could make but little improvement in it. My first work next winter will be to go through very carefully, with my most valued assistant from Rupert's House, all I have written this winter. Every word will be examined, and wherever an improvement can be made it will be made; and then the New Testament will come under review, and then I trust one of the principal works of my life will be accomplished, my most cherished hope realised—my people will have the Word of God in a form they can thoroughly understand.'

In June, 1892, the bishop visited Rupert's House, and, still full of energy and indefatigable in his work, had scarcely returned when he prepared to start off on a much longer trip to Whale River and Fort George.

On the eve of setting off he wrote, alluding to the arrival of a 'packet' with letters and papers:

'Just think of seven months of reviews and missionary publications, as well as other periodicals, coming at one time, and that the busiest time of the year, when every minute must be utilised for work. The consequence is that many papers are never opened at all. It is sometimes a question with me as to whether this is a gain or a loss; it certainly keeps my mind fixed on my work, of which there is always a great deal more to be done than can be well got through. You good people at home cannot at all realise our position ; we are in another world, and you have the same difficulty in endeavouring to realise it as you would have in realising the condition of life in the planet Mars.

'On Saturday last I returned from Rupert's House, having with me my daughter, Mrs. Broughton, her husband, and family. They will now live at Moose, Mr. Broughton having been appointed to the charge of the whole southern department. At present they are staying with me, but next week they go to the Factory, five minutes' walk from my house, which will then be vacated by its present occupants, who are returning to Canada. To-morrow I set off for Fort George and Whale River, Mr. Peck's district. I shall be absent about a month, and trust that in that time I may be able to do much for the Master. We are passing through the hottest summer known here for many years; the heat is sometimes almost unbearable, while the mosquitoes are most venomous and annoying. Our gardens look well so far, and we hope to have good crops by-and-by.'

In August the bishop was back at Moose Fort. 'I am once more in the old house,' he writes, 'home from my long summer journeyings, and I don't think I shall leave it again this year, but employ myself in my usual educational and translation duties. I first went to Whale River, which receives its name from the large number of porpoises found there: there was formerly a great trade in the oil produced from them as well as in their skins. I started from Moose in the Mink schooner on July 15. We had foul winds, and the cold became severe, and many icebergs were about, which occasionally gave our vessel some heavy blows. Then we passed the Twins, two large islands of equal size, on which grows neither tree nor shrub; then we caught sight of Cape Jones, which divides James' Bay from Hudson's Bay, and Bear Island, a large, high rock of most forbidding aspect; and then we ran along Long Island, which has a very bad repute as the centre of the abode of storms, and as we pass it the great tors on the mainland rise one after the other in their majesty of desolation; and there is more ice, and more islands, and an abundance of fog, hiding everything from view. And here, at last, is the south point of the river, and presently we come to anchor, for the wind will not allow us to proceed up to the Hudson's Bay Company's establishment; but a canoe is soon alongside, and in that I am taken ashore, and am presently among those who have been eagerly looking for me, and who receive me with a warm welcome. There is much work to do, and I am alone.

'Our first service on Sunday commences at half-past six in the morning: all the Indians at the place are present, and all seem to enjoy it; some among the congregation I have not seen for years. They had wandered off to Ungava, many hundreds of miles distant, and had long remained there; they now say that they intend to make Whale River their permanent trading post. We take breakfast, and then for our Eskimo service. You see before you a goodly number of clean, intelligent-looking people, short and stout; you see that they have books in their hands, and notice that they readily find out the places required; they sing very nicely, having greatly improved since my last visit to them. Thank God for the blessing He has vouchsafed to the missionaries' labour. And now we attend the English service. One young person is confirmed, and three partake of the Lord's Supper. After this we have dinner; this finished, it will soon be time for our second Indian service, so let us walk quietly to the house we use as a church. It is already crowded with young and old; all sing the sweet Indian hymns, and use the Church prayers in their Indian dress. I baptize twelve children and perform four marriages. The Indians retire, and soon the interesting Eskimo flock in and take their places; two people are confirmed, and four partake of the sacrament. We are all a little tired now, the more so from the atmosphere being very close in the church; so we go up to the top of the extensive plain on which are pitched the Indian and Eskimo tents, and take a brisk walk among the heather, which gives us an appetite for tea. On the table is tea, preserved milk, sugar, bread, and marrow fat. Our last service is afterwards held; the old familiar English one. We have had a busy day, and yet not quite so busy as it would have been at Churchill, on the western side of the bay, where, in addition to the three languages spoken here, we should have had the Chipwyan. We have a little conversation and then go to bed, for we must be early astir to-morrow morning.

'Yes, in the morning there was a great stir: all hands were up at four o'clock, loading the schooner, which had taken everything in by six o'clock, when I held my last service, the last in all probability I shall ever hold at Whale River. I then had breakfast, after which, having said good-bye to and shaken hands with every one—English, half-caste, Indian and Eskimo—I hastened on board. The anchor was at once raised, and we began to descend the river amidst volley after volley of musketry, the Indians wishing to testify their appreciation of what had been attempted for their good.

'After we had left the river we bent our way southward, and went as fast as the baffling winds would allow us. We had the high rocky coast on our left, on which side lay Long Island; then we passed Bear Island and Cape Jones, and Lucker Creek and Wastekan Island, the highest land between Cape Jones and Fort George, and Governor's Island, and Horse Island, and others, and so came to the mouth of Fort George River. We were seen at the fort, when instantly the flag was run up. On and on we went until we arrived opposite the landing-place, when the anchor was dropped and a boat took me ashore. I was directly in the midst of old and warm friends, who gave me the heartiest of welcomes.

'I was eight days at Fort George, and they were all busy ones. I kept school twice a day, devoting the mornings to the Indian children and the afternoons to those speaking English. I held likewise two services each day, one in each language, and for the few days that some Eskimo were at the place, one for them as well. The principal Eskimo here is called Nero, and he is really a fine fellow, about the size of a big English boy, although I think the English boy would have but little chance with him in a wrestling match. I got him to assist me in one of the services, and what he did he did well.

'The Indians are all busy haymaking. They go up the river some distance, and there find abundance of grass, and bring it down in boats, spreading it on a large field, where they make it into hay. There are stables for the cattle, but there are no horses. There are four or five houses for the workpeople, and on a large plain are some Indian tents—and the gardens are looking well—the potatoes and turnips look as if good crops would be secured, a matter for congratulation, as this is by no means always the case. Day follows day, and the last arrived, when I gave a treat to all the children.

'Our farewell service is held, and it is a very solemn one, for every one at Fort George is very dear to me. I wish all and everyone good-bye, for I start early on the morrow; but early as it is, everyone is on the river's bank to see me as I step into a large canoe, which is to take me seven miles to the Mink, lying in Stromness harbour. Several farewell volleys are fired, and I am speedily out of sight of my hospitable friends and on my way to the old house at Moose.'

To the bishop's great joy and thankfulness a young missionary, Mr. Walton, arrived by the ship in the autumn of 1892. He was destined for the distant post of Ungava. The bishop was much pleased with him, and, after due examination, ordained him, and sent him on to Fort George to fill meanwhile the place of Mr. Peck, who was by doctor's advice to take his wife and children to England by the ship homeward bound.

Mr. Peck would, the bishop hoped, return in the following May, to proceed to Ungava with the Rev. W. Walton.

The journey to Ungava is toilsome and very difficult. Mr. Peck had visited the post in 1885, having been driven back three times before he succeeded in crossing the Labrador peninsula, eight hundred miles. He was repaid at length by meeting with many Eskimo anxious for the message of salvation. The thought of the pressing need for a missionary to this far-off spot had ever since lain 'heavy on the heart of the bishop.' He said, 'If we go to the North Pole, we shall be still in the diocese of Moosonee.' The ice-bound regions visited by Sir John Franklin, Admiral McClintock, Captain Parry, and other Arctic explorers, are nearly all in this diocese.

The bishop worked on, assisted by the Rev. J. A. Newnham, who had returned from a visit to Montreal, bringing with him a wife, who took the deepest interest in the women and girls, and proved a great addition to the mission party. The native pastor, the Rev. E. Richards, was also staying at Moose at this time, especially to help in the revision of the Bible translations.

CHAPTER XXI

LAST DAYS

TOWARDS the end of November the bishop was taken suddenly ill. We have the account of his attack in his own words, written on January 2, 1893, by his daughter Chrissie from his dictation. 'Three-and-fifty years ago Christmas was spent by me in bed; my life was almost given up. I was suffering from typhus fever, and my doctor said that, had I not had a constitution of lead, I must have succumbed to the virulence of the disease. God raised me up again, and eventually sent me to the land of snow, and I am now spending my forty-second Christmas in connection with it. And how very joyous every Christmas has been up to the present one! How wonderfully good my health has always been, how I could always join the frolic and fun of the youngsters! I felt as one of them; the difference in our age was as nothing. We were all children. This year, too, the church has been beautifully decorated; the splendid trees have been laden with their precious fruits, faces have brightened with joy as of yore: but I have seen nothing of them; the mingled voices of childhood have been unheard

'It has been God's will that I should spend this Christmas in a sick room, and amid much and severe suffering. He has brought down my strength in my journey; but amidst it all He has kept me in perfect peace. On November 20 I was very well. I preached at both English and Indian services, and took my class in the Indian school, spending the evening with my dear daughter and her family. I was in bed by ten, and arose on Monday, November 21, before it was daylight, according to custom, for I had a great work on hand, and about a quarter after seven, when the light had become sufficiently strong, I went on with my revision of the New Testament in the Cree language. I commenced the twelfth chapter of St. Luke, and worked on steadily for a quarter of an hour, when I suddenly felt as if I had received a very heavy blow in the lower portion of my back. I knew it was a stroke of rheumatism, but rheumatism was a companion of many years' standing—not a pleasant one by any means, but it had never materially interfered with my work. So, thinking that this was merely a twinge of a rather more severe character than usual, I continued my labour; but soon stroke after stroke succeeded of a more and more violent nature. I sat up until after prayers and breakfast, and then was conducted to bed, which I reached with great difficulty; severe torturing pains, the nature of which I had hitherto no conception of, came on with every movement.

'For a week I could do nothing, although my general health had not much suffered. I then, however, resumed the revision of my last winter's work on the Cree Old Testament, devoting some hours to it every day, assisted by my most valuable helper. the Rev. E. Richards. In a few days more I trust that the whole of the Old Testament will be fit for the printer's hands; I shall then go on with the New Testament, and, God helping me, I hope to see it completed in the summer. Picture me in my work. I am lying on my back in my bed; Mr. Richards is sitting at a table by my side; I have my English Bible, the Revised Version, in my hand; Mr. Richards has my translation before him, which he is reading to me slowly and distinctly. Every sentence is very carefully weighed, and all errors are corrected. This is a glorious occupation, and I cannot feel too thankful that I am able to follow it in these days of my weakness.

'I am much better than I was, and I trust it will not be long before I shall be able to be about as usual. But it was almost worth while to be visited with this affliction, to experience the loving and anxious care of every one by whom I am surrounded. Everyone does his and her best to alleviate my sufferings. Our medical man has done his very utmost; a kind and loving daughter, and her equally kind husband and children, Mr. and Mrs. Newnham, Mr. and Mrs. Richards, and all my Indian and native friends, have vied with each other in administering to my comfort.'

The end of February, the date at which the bishop expected his budget of news from the outer world, brought to his friends in England the sad tidings that he had died suddenly on January 12. The telegram had been carried four hundred miles to Matawa, the nearest post-office. In due course letters followed. The end had come very unexpectedly to those about him.

The Rev. J. A. Newnham wrote: 'Our dear bishop has entered into rest—a more perfect rest than that which he expected to enjoy later in the year. It seems to have been failure of the heart which caused his death. . . . The people of Moosonee, and of Moose Factory especially, have lost a father, a loving friend, and are plunged in grief. . . . The remains, clad in episcopal robes, and laid in the coffin, were placed in the church awaiting the funeral, and the people, young and old, all came to take a last farewell of the face so dear to them, and of one who had been in and out of their houses, cottages, and wigwams for over forty years, as a missionary, pastor, friend, and bishop. . . . Archdeacon Vincent arrived on the evening of the 20th. On the 21st, Saturday, the coffin was closed in the presence of four clergymen—the Rev. W. G. Walton having arrived with the dogs from Fort George—and of the gentlemen of the Honourable Hudson's Bay Company from Fort George, Rupert's House, and Albany, as well as Moose Fort.

'At three P.M. the burial service was read, and the body of the first Bishop of Moosonee was reverently committed to the grave. It was a beautiful afternoon, almost spring-like, and the whole adult population was present in the church and at the grave. Thus our bishop, amid the tears of his bereaved people, was laid to rest, as he had said he would have wished, in the midst of his flock.'

At the time of his death Bishop Horden had just attained the age of sixty-five. He had been forty-two years in the field. He had laboured in the apostolic spirit with a large measure of apostolic success. He had laid well and deeply, building upon the Rock which is Christ, the foundation of the work in that vast district. This is being continued by men trained under his influence, and fired by his example. Denied the brief season of earthly rest to which he had looked forward, he has entered the sooner into the perfect rest above. He has ceased from his labours and for us it is to strive and pray that the flock which he so long and faithfully shepherded in Moosonee shall at length be brought to join him in the heavenly fold above.